THE PICTURE PALACE

Excursions into Architecture

Series editors
John Smith
David Braithwaite

THE PICTURE PALACE

and other buildings
for the movies

Dennis Sharp

Hugh Evelyn London

First published in 1969
by Hugh Evelyn Limited
9 Fitzroy Square, London W1

© 1969 Dennis Sharp

238 78885 7

Designed by Sheila Sherwen

Printed and bound in the
Republic of Ireland
by Hely Thom Limited

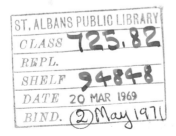

Contents

for Melanie Clare

Enter the dreamhouse, brothers and sisters, leaving
Your debts asleep, your history at the door:
This is the home for heroes, and this loving
Darkness a fur you can afford

C. Day Lewis, from *Newsreel* c 1938

Introduction

In its relatively short history the picture palace—or the motion picture house as it was known in its heyday in the United States—has gone through many changes. At the turn of the century there was not a building in the world devoted exclusively to cinematograph use; thirty or forty years later cinemas could be found in almost every major city or town. 'Movie madness' spread around the world like a fireball. Buildings for the movies became a common part of the urban scene, characterised by their size, distinctive frontages and external lettering.

The first cinema programmes were presented in music halls, finding a place between the turns. Films at this stage were short and silent. Expansion of the embryonic film industry came through the introduction of shop shows and fairground booths to house a growing and endlessly inquisitive film-going public. The entrance fee to the converted shop premises was usually a penny in Britain, hence the generic term 'the penny gaff'; patrons paid a nickel in the States and the premises were known as 'nickelodeons'. In the East End of London a few promotors allowed kids to enter on the production of jam-jars—a two-pounder was worth a penny.

The first cinema buildings were simply derived from the conventional theatre or music hall and usually included a plain auditorium, a stage area—this time for turns between the films—with a piano, a pavement paybox and entrance hall and a small bar for the sale of confections.

The super cinema (and the American movie palace) followed the introduction of the talkies. These were much more ambitious buildings, still essentially an extension of the conventional theatre, but with more pomp in the entrance hall and foyer, elaborate lighting effects and ambitious decorative schemes in the auditorium. The Wurlitzer organ replaced the wheezy piano and ballrooms and restaurants were added.

The American movie palaces of the twenties acted as models on which British and European designers drew for inspiration. Basically there were two schools of thought about movie buildings in the States, one advocated the use of neo-Classical forms and motifs and was known as the 'hard-top' school, the other advocated a more experimental type of structure where a completely artificial environment could be created and was known as the 'atmospheric' school. Thomas W. Lamb was the doyen of the first group of designers and was firmly rooted in the *Beaux-Arts* tradition. John Eberson inspired the more bizarre designs of the atmospherics. In between there were the designers who would conceive their buildings as the mood took them or the promotor dictated.

In the twenties British architects such as Frank Verity and Robert Atkinson displayed their allegiance to the Lamb school. Verity's Shepherd's Bush Pavilion which opened in 1924 was quaintly neo-Classical—like many of the town halls of the period—and gained an RIBA medal for architectural merit. A decade later, during the boom years for the British cinema, architects were torn between a desire for the restraints and respectability of Classical detailing and the urge for a new type of façade that would reflect the uniqueness of the film medium. No one succeeded more than Harry W. Weedon, the Birmingham architect, in establishing a distinctive and consistent form of expression for modern movie buildings. His many Odeons owed little stylistically to any previous examples and were usually designed with a vertical feature, finished in faience panels, and possessed a quality that American car producers referred to as 'streamlining'. Only when his buildings were situated in historic towns were they modified and then quite specifically in the Amsterdam School brickwork style.

Designing buildings for the movies demanded (and indeed still demands) a considerable number of skills. Although each building may be attributed to a single architect or to a firm and the result seen as an imaginative interpretation of the client's requirements it is worth remembering that the most successful buildings were the product of an inter-professional team. The architect, the structural engineer, the heating and ventilating expert, the acoustics consultant and the interior decorator all had their part to play in the design of the building.

The picture palace is a distinctly twentieth-century building type together with structures for transport, communications, modern engineering, science and the like. As its precedents are in the theatre and the fairground this undoubtedly has hindered designers in finding original solutions and adequate means of expression for the new building type. Even with the expected short life of cinema buildings and a few attempts at standardisation (some American companies shipped out complete cinemas to countries with inadequate building resources in the twenties and thirties) each one was tailor-made for its location and usually constructed according to traditional methods. Most cinemas had a simple external appearance, except for the show façade, with undecorated backs and sides. The special treatment given to the frontages evolved directly from the fairground booths and the biograph shows. Promoters who had moved in on the new mass media had been brought up with a desire for an ostentatious display at the front of their 'houses' and they passed on this same enthusiasm to the designers. What the public wants it gets, the philosophy of the early promoters seems to have been, forgetting momentarily that they had been responsible for introducing the paraphernalia of cinema presentation in the first place. Too often in the past the paying public have been at the receiving end of a grotesque mixture of styles and decorative details more appropriate to the fun fair, the music hall and the gin palace than to the synthetic world of motion pictures where sight lines, ample circulation space, seating comfort and auditorium size were the key factors.

The movie demanded a new type of building; it can hardly be claimed that it got it. Most of the innovations in the cinema have been confined to the technical side of film production, to image size and screen size, to the development of sound and vision techniques and to presentation gimmicks. The building used to house the presentation of a programme of films has too often in the past been considered irrelevant. Indeed any research that was necessary to the development of cinema building was done in the boom years by the busy architect who was far too occupied with meeting building dates to gain much from a wider consideration of his problems. He drew his initial inspiration from previous examples and carried out his own investigations into the design problems on a strictly *ad hoc* basis. It is little wonder that many draughty, ill-ventilated and badly designed interiors have fallen into disfavour with the general public. The decline in the cinema in Britain since 1945 is usually attributed to the advances made in television and home entertainments and promoters have been scratching their commercial heads to find a solution to this problem. Paradoxically they have aggravated the situation in their endeavour to monopolise the industry by reducing the number of cinema buildings—without much consideration whether the buildings were good or bad—and by introducing block bookings of films for cinemas in one area (giving little choice to the cinema-goer) as well as featuring second rate supporting films and corny advertisements. Under 2,000 cinemas remain in operation in Britain and while it is said that this figure represents an economic balance for the industry there is little doubt that the marked increase of interest in the cinema art over the last few years can only be met by experimentation with new presentation, new forms of enclosure and ultimately a new cinema architecture.

The building of new cinemas and the re-vamping of older buildings that is going on today appears pathetically inadequate to meet the requirements for visual and aural excitement at the entertainment level and for the expanding needs for education and instruction. In order that this vital medium can expand and design innovations take place the promoters should be encouraged to see that the design of cinemas is a complex and exacting task that cannot be entrusted to the inexperienced designers they often employ to renovate buildings for bingo and bowling alleys. In this study I have tried to pin-point a few of the problems and to indicate some of the complexities of cinema design.

I have also attempted to analyse both visually and technically a number of significant examples and to place them within the context of the whole development of cinema building. Facts have been hard to come by as the unassembled skeleton of the history of movie architecture is to be found not in previous books nor in the archives of the film companies, but largely in the technical and specialist periodicals and in the memories of architects and promoters who were responsible for individual buildings.

From much reading and searching and from numerous conversations with the people who were involved one point becomes very clear; cinema buildings for critics of contemporary architecture and for the purists in the mainstream of the Modern Movement were considered to be not quite architecture. Even with their streamline styling they were not acceptably 'modern'—built as they were in a period when architects were searching for functional and geometric integrity—nor were they a respectable building type to the socially minded designer. I trust that this study will redress the balance in favour of those architects who have contributed something to a difficult and complex form of building. Perhaps also, and I do not intend to be too subjective in print, they may have contributed to the art of building.

Dennis Sharp
St Albans

Authors acknowledgements

I am greatly indebted to the many people, architects, promotors, managers, film critics, writers and the oddly assorted collection of individuals who call themselves cinema building enthusiasts who helped me in my researches for this book. Since starting the text in 1965 I have been amazed at the amount of interest that has been shown in the project and gratified with the amount of new and largely unpublished material that has come to light.

While it would be impossible to mention everyone by name I would like to thank Mr Robert Cromie especially for providing me with a great deal of information on the cinema architects of the 'thirties and on his own work, and also for reading through, and commenting on, the proofs; Mr Hall of Harry Weedon and Partners for information on the practical issues that cinema design raised; to the late Julian Leathart; to Mr Chetwood of Drury, Gomersall and Partners for an account of cinema building in the north of England; and Cecil Young and Partners.

I also wish to acknowledge my gratitude to the following for advice, guidance and help with illustrations; the Director of the British Lighting Council; Brian Pearce of Pearce Signs Ltd; Percy Corry; Keith Hodkinson; Graham Nowell of the Motion Picture Theatre Library; the Duckworth family; Francis A. Mangan; John Adams of Cassidy, Farrington and Dennys; E. Callenbach, Editor, *Film Quarterly*, and John Kobal. My thanks also go to Ben Hall, the author of *The Best Remaining Seats* for providing some very useful information and giving permission through his publisher Clarkson N. Potter, Inc, to use copyright material from that book © MCMLXI by Ben Hall; to W. G. Altria, Editor of *Kine Weekly* for the opportunity to look through the archives of that journal; to Ian Cameron, Editor, *Movie* magazine for continual advice and encouragement; to Mr Ronald Wigg of Adelaide for advice on acoustics and early Australian cinemas; to John Lander of the RIBA; Ernö Goldfinger, Douglas Cole, N. Ritchie and David Braithwaite. John Smith, the co-editor of the series, has performed his editorial responsibilities with his usual diligence and skill and as always his enthusiasm and knowledge has made the task of the author so much easier.

I also express my thanks to the following organisations for help with factual information and illustrations: The Library of the Royal Institute of British Architects, the Architectural Association, the public libraries in Manchester, Sheffield, Liverpool, Glasgow and Hull, the Rank Organisation, Granada Ltd, Paramount Film Service Ltd, BBC, Hans Rohr, Zurich, The Radio Times Hulton Picture Library, Cleveland Engineering Co, Colne, the National Film Archive, the Nederlands Filmmuseum, the National Monuments Record, Philips of Eindhoven and The Strand Electric and Engineering Company. My publishers and I wish to acknowledge William Heinemann Ltd for permission to use a quotation from their book *New York* by Paul Morand, Jonathan Cape, The Hogarth Press and Harold Matson Co, Inc, for permission to use the verse from 'Newsreel' by C. Day Lewis from *Collected Poems 1965*.

I thank my wife for her valuable comments on the text and for doing most of the work involved in producing the selected list of cinemas at the end of the book.

Dennis Sharp, 1965–

Sources of the illustrations

Every care has been taken to ensure proper acknowledgement to the copyright holders of photographs, drawings and models but in many cases the material has been handed on second or third hand. As a result the names of original owners or photographers have in some cases been lost. The illustrations not listed come from the author's own collection. The illustrations are listed by page numbers.

Akademie der Künste, Berlin, 153 (top), 156, 158-9 (top)
The Architectural Association, London, 153 (bottom)
Architects' Journal, 196-7
The Architectural Press, 208
Ernest Callenbach, Esq, 203 (4)
Cleveland Engineering Co, Colne, 50 (right)
Douglas P. Cole, 58 (left), 59 (bottom), 90, 98, 105, 108-9, 110 (left), 113 (bottom), 121, 146 (top), 192 (2)
P. Colomb, Esq, colour plate 1
Robert Cromie, Esq, endpapers, 107 (2), 167 (2)
Drury, Gomersall and Partners, 52 (top), 87-8, 120, 122-3, 124-5, 127, 164 (top), 172-3, 174-5
The Duckworth Family, 50 (left)
Ernö Goldfinger, Esq, 200-1
Ben Hall, Esq (used by permission of Clarkson Potter Inc, New York), 72 (2), 78-9, 80-1
William R. Heick, 82-4, colour plate 4

Keith Hodkinson, Esq, 54, 59 (top), 89 (bottom), 145, 204
Cecil Howitt and Partners, 141 (top)
The late Julian Leathart, Esq, 95-7, 164 (bottom), 166 (2)
Manchester Central Library, 170-1, 181, 182
National Buildings Record, London, 40-1, 45 (top), 53, 56-7, 60-1, 64-5, 67 (2), 68
National Film Archive, London, 29, 30-1, 32 (top), 33, 39 (bottom), 42, 45, 46, 47, 71, 75, 77, 102, 111, 113 (top), 115, 116, 117, 142-3, 149-50, 179
Nederlands Filmmuseum, 43 (2), 44 (2), 48
Cas Oorthuys, Esq, 185
Pearce Signs Ltd, 143 (bottom)
A. I. Percival, Esq, 51 (2)
Radio Times Hulton Picture Library, London, 16, 18, 19 (2), 20-21, 22 (2), 24, 25, 27, 42, 146 (bottom), 146-7
The Rank Organisation, 67 (left), 34-5, 118-9, 141, 193, 198-9, 205, 206 (2)
The Royal Institute of British Architects, 159, 190 (2)
Sheffield Newspapers Ltd, 63
Eric Thompson, Esq, 194
Harry W. Weedon and Partners, 129, 130-1, 132-3, 134-5, 136-7, 138-9, 144
Mrs H. Wigg, 160
Ronald Wigg, Esq, 58 (2)
Ian Yeomans, Esq, colour plates 2, 3

1

Buildings of the
pre-movie era

Left **A Phantasmagoria Lantern
used by Etienne Gaspard
Robertson**
Opposite **One of Mr Robertson's
famous delusions 'The Dance of
the Demons' using candlelights
as a source to obtain double
images onto a screen. The picture
below shows an audience reaction
to the Phantasmagoria**

The film industry was born during the last decade of the
nineteenth century. It emerged as a commercial enterprise
almost apologetically and in rather humble surroundings.
Tied as it was to the inventor's table it seems incredible to
us nowadays that the first moving films were one man shows
peeped at through the eye-hole of a machine. Few people—
certainly not Edison and his colleagues at the time—could
have predicted that the moving picture machine, the Kinetoscope, would later graduate into the super-movie palace
seating anything up to 5,000 people.

It was the demand from the public to see the novelty of
animated pictures that forced the inventors to convert the
viewing box into a projection apparatus. That took some
considerable time. In the pre-movie era the science of optics
had fascinated the inventors. They had been quick to ob-
serve the popularity the effects of illusion had with the
general public. By the second half of the nineteenth century
projected illusions had become part of the stock-in-trade of
many theatres. The illusionistic tricks had come to the stage
through the *prestidigitateur* and his magic lantern.

The magic lantern itself—a simple box that houses a lamp
and two convex lenses—was a seventeenth century invention. It was the magic lantern in its perfected form, as a
phantasmagoria, that introduced a paying public to a projected picture. It was used by E G Robertson as a spectacular
form of public entertainment in Paris at the turn of the
eighteenth century. Robertson projected his images on to a
calico screen from behind creating a mysterious and spectral

effect. In F Marion's book, *The Wonders of Optics* (London
1868), an account is given of Robertson's exhibition room
which suggests that it was a direct fore-runner of the cinema
auditorium.

'In order to obtain the best results he used a room some
sixty or eighty feet long, and twenty-four wide, which he
hung entirely with black. Of this a strip twenty-five feet long
was cut off and devoted to the manipulation of the phanta-
magoria. This portion of the apartment was separated from
the spectators by a white calico screen, tightly strained from
side to side, and at first concealed from view by a black
curtain. The calico screen, which was about twenty feet
square, was well soaked in a mixture of starch and fine gum
arabic, in order to render it semi-transparent. The floor was
raised about four or five feet at one end in order that the
whole of the spectators might have a free and uninterrupted
view of what was going on.'

The total illusion was heightened by the effect of the
lantern moving backwards and forwards by means of a rack
and pinion and also through a movable diaphragm that
increased or decreased the aperture at will. With this added
facility Robertson brought his ghost dramas to life and
frightened his audiences to death. Robertson held his first
public *séance* in an apartment in the *Pavillon de l'échiquier*
in Paris. His audience amounted to between sixty and
seventy people. How intimate the performances were is
reflected in the description of an eyewitness:

'At seven o'clock a pale thin man (Robertson) entered the

room where we were sitting, and having extinguished the candles he said: "Citizens and gentlemen, I am not one of those adventurers and impudent swindlers who promise more than they can perform. I have assured the public in the *Journal de Paris* that I can bring the dead to life, and I shall do so. Those of the company who desire to see the apparitions of those who were dear to them, but who have passed away . . . have only to speak, and I shall obey their commands".'

On this occasion, the eye-witness goes on, Robertson obliged with a resurrection of Marat, the evocation of William Tell and an appearance of Virgil, among others. But probably the most amusing incident occurred when a young man asked to see the phantom of 'a young lady he tenderly loved'. After taking a look at her photograph, Robertson threw on the brazier—conveniently situated in front of the screen—a few sparrow's feathers, a grain or two of phosphorus and a dozen butterflies. Let the commentator finish:

'A beautiful woman, with her bosom uncovered and her hair floating about her, soon appeared, and smiled at the young man with the most tender regard and sorrow. A grave-looking individual sitting close by me suddenly exclaimed, "Heavens! its my wife come to life again", and rushed from the room, apparently fearing that it was not a phantom.'

After that particular night the exhibition was prohibited by the authorities and Robertson's equipment sealed. But it was soon to open again, this time in the eery atmosphere of an old Capucin convent chapel near the Place Vendôme.

The Robertson room layout gave an indication of the use of space for projected images, but it was the later buildings developed for such recent innovations as the panorama and the diorama that engendered a distinctive form. The buildings, taking the name of the inventions as a description of their type, were auditoria inside where the spectacle took place. The panorama was suggested by the German painter of architectural scenes, Breizig, and later made practicable and first exhibited by a Scottish artist and inventor, Robert Barker, in Edinburgh in 1788. It was a simple enough idea. Barker conceived a presentation of a series of paintings on curved surfaces which a spectator could view from a central position. He undertook such a painting representing Edinburgh from Carlton Hill, patented the idea and after an initial run brought his invention to the Haymarket in March 1789. It was an immediate success, even though ridiculed by such an eminent man as Sir Joshua Reynolds.

In 1793 Barker opened a new building devoted exclusively to the panorama in Leicester Square. The plan of the building consisted of three circular areas. The largest unit was a cylinder ninety feet in diameter and forty feet high. The Panorama presented contemporary war scenes, public ceremonials, and scenes of spectacular natural beauty.

From London the panorama spread to Paris where two rotundas were built as annexes to the classical *Théâtre des Variétés* on the Boulevard Montmartre. Soon the novel

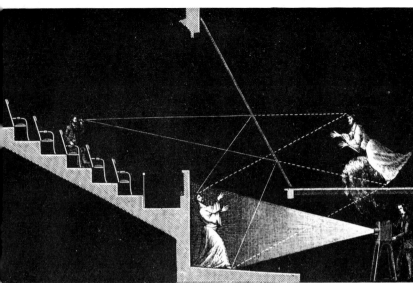

Left **Section of the phantom show**

Below **The method employed to produce ghosts by M. Robin at his exhibition in the Boulevard du Temple**

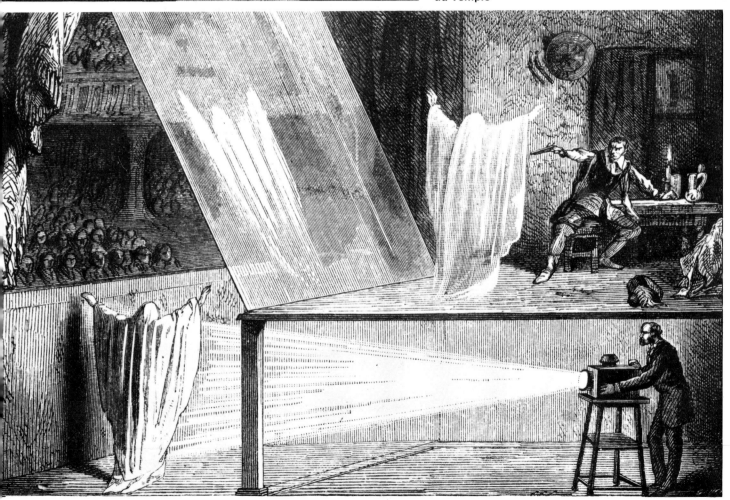

Above **The exterior of James Thyer's two Panorama rotundas on the Boulevard Montmartre, Paris, 1800**

Opposite **The Diorama and the interior of a Camera Obscura**

was to be found in most major cities in Europe. The buildin was much the same in each case. The Rotunda in Liverpool fashionable Bold Street was a typical example, with a conic roof and a central shaft around which the panorama move It was taken down in 1864. Burford's Leicester Squa Panorama (Burford had succeeded Robert Barker ar Barker's son as the owner) remained a popular form entertainment for nearly 70 years. Elsewhere, it was soc superseded by the Diorama. This was a considerable re finement of the type of presentation seen in the panoram It combined the use of large paintings and pictorial view with changing scenic and optical effects produced by mag lanterns and translucent colours.

The new technique was introduced by the famous Frenc inventor Louis Daguerre in conjunction with Bouton. The opened their first Diorama in the Rue Sanson, Paris, in 182 In this building the auditorium revolved around the giar scenery and the spectator viewed parts of the scene throug an opening in the auditorium wall shaped somewhat like conventional proscenium opening. Later examples adopte

The Diorama, Regent's Park

the less expensive approach with the scene viewed from a distance through the opening and a diversity of scenic effect produced by using shutters and screens. Again the Liverpool example that existed in Bold Street was typical.

Daguerre brought his invention to London in the 1820s and established a Diorama in John Nash's Park Square East terrace, Regent's Park, which was built during 1823. The rotunda salon, situated at the back of the terrace, was designed by Augustus Charles Pugin to form part of the building. The shell still exists today and so do the steps to the main foyer, but no vestige remains of the diorama itself which was destroyed by fire in 1839.

Probably the finest and certainly the most adventurous

Diorama in London was the one built for 'Mr Wylde, tl geographer' in Leicester Square Gardens in 1851. Aft erecting his 'Great Globe' Mr Wylde found himself in ambiguous position from a legal point of view. Having pu chased, as he thought, the fee simple of the garden he lat had to comply with a restrictive provision that after t years he would have to remove his building and restore tl railings to the garden. In fact his Great Globe did stand f the statutory ten years on the site of one of London's be known public open spaces. The Great Globe itself was six feet in diameter and filled most of the building with its hu; domed roof designed especially for it by the archite Abrahams. The building was centrally positioned witl

Above **Wylde's Great Globe,
Leicester Square Gardens**

Left **Cross-section through the
Great Globe**

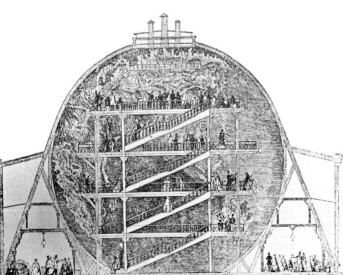

Above **Mr Albert Smith presenting
his programme 'The ascent of
Mont Blanc' at the Egyptian Hall**

Right **The Egyptian Hall,
Piccadilly, 1823**

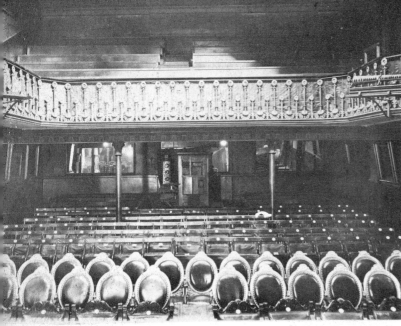

the Square and four smaller exhibition halls were situate
off the main centre lines.

Of all the pre-movie buildings in London of the nin
teenth century the Egyptian Hall, situated on the south si
of Piccadilly, was one of the most distinctive. It was erecte
in 1812 by Edward Bullock and designed to accommoda
a museum of natural history and Egyptology. The archite
responsible for the main facade was P F Robinson. With i
Egyptian detailing this facade was to set a fashion f
architects in this country as well as abroad. Later, after t
'Egyptian' had become a permanent home for animate
pictures, it was a fashion that was to inspire a number
buildings for the new form of entertainment. The Hall w
replaced in 1905 by Egyptian House.

Subsequently, with the introduction of moving pictur
in the late nineteenth century it became obvious that a ne
type of building would eventually emerge to accommoda
the unique invention and its inquisitive patrons. The d
cade that followed, in which an embryonic industry and
new sophisticated form of entertainment were seeking
home, was a confused one. The film moved from place
place, from its temporary home in the Music Hall to the fai
ground; from the rented hall to the converted shop. Eac
new home brought its problems and frustrations, but durir
the early stages of the history of film it only mattered if th
promoters could 'pack them in' and make a penny or tw
The temporary 'house' then was as uncertain of success
the picture palace in the days immediately after the last wa

2

From the kinetoscope
parlour to
the nickelodeon

dison's Latest Invention: The Kinetoscope'. This small
otice was to be found on the top of each of the magic boxes
at stood like up-turned coffins in the Holland Brothers'
musement arcade on Broadway in 1894. Outside, the
ieues formed and the patrons trooped in to view the first
hibition of motion pictures. Edison's (really his assistant
ickson's) invention was at first operated by the arcade
oprietor, who took money at the door and started each
achine individually. Later the machines were operated by
simple nickel-in-the-slot mechanism. They required little
ore than standing space. The peep-hole machine con-
sted of an upright wooden box with a front hinged door.
ithin the box a wooden panel carried a series of reels of
rious diameters around which a forty or fifty-foot endless
nd of film was threaded. The viewer at the top of the box
oked directly onto a magnifying lens through which each
nage of film could be seen.

It had been originally anticipated that the first Kine-
oscope machines (the very first one had been produced in
891) and films would be ready for the Chicago World Fair
1893, but Edison had been busy on other things and in
e end was unable to fulfill his earlier promise. Contrary to
any accounts it was not until May 1894 that the first
eep-show parlour opened in Chicago.

Although the Kinetoscope was the seed-box of the
otion picture, it failed to sustain the interest it had at first
ngendered and after a brief period of success in the nickel
arlours it was soon reduced to a fairground novelty. Even

Opposite **Lumière's cinémaographe
projector, 1896, from an engraving
by Poyet**

its inventors failed to grasp fully its potential as the fore-runner of projected motion pictures. It was left to other inventors to bring the marriage of moving film to the projected image.

The news of Edison's invention travelled far and wide and throughout the world attempts were made almost simultaneously to turn the machine into projection apparatus. Robert Paul's attempts in London to convert a Kinetoscope were not successful at first but his experiments eventually led to success early in 1895. In his Hatton Garden studio he produced, to his profound amazement, a projected picture seven feet square—animated and reasonably clear.

Throughout Europe similar experiments were taking place and fascinating as the accounts of these are, it is unnecessary here to join in the arguments about which inventor or nation has prior claim. The story of the work carried out by American, British, German and French inventors may be found elsewhere. It is, however, necessary to put into proper perspective at this stage the commercial side of the cinema and to establish a date order for the beginnings of the industry for which a completely new building type had to be fashioned. In the latter half of the nineties, paying public performances began to take place in well-known and fashionable *rendezvous*.

Following a number of private showings the Skladanowsky Brothers projected 'intermittent photographs' taken on Eastman film with their Bioscope (double projector) in the Wintergarten, Berlin, in November 1895. In December o the same year the Lumière Brothers gave their first publi performance of moving pictures (again after a series o private showings) in the Grand Café on the Boulevard de Capucines, Paris. These shows continued for some time an the extent of public interest they caused can be judged b the takings, which on the first day were 35 francs but whic increased to 300 francs daily soon afterwards. The Lumièr Brothers immediately patented their equipment.

According to C W Ceram it went under the title o '*Kinetoscope de (en) projection*' but was later retitled *Cinéma tographie*—a word which has been retained to this day i French and English in the abbreviated version of the titl for a cinematograph theatre: Cinema.

The ingenious apparatus invented by the Lumieres wa demonstrated in England at the Regent Street Polytechni in February 1896 under the direction of Professor Trewe (Treuwé). The whole show was transferred to the ol Empire Music Hall, Leicester Square, in March of tha year. Also in March, after an earlier private exhibition a Finsbury Technical College and at the Royal Institute Robert Paul introduced his 'Theatrograph' to the genera public at Olympia. It was an immediate success. Olympi became the first independent picture showplace in England The public demand for this new and novel medium ha been predicted by Sir Augustus Harris, then the owner o Olympia, after he had seen Paul's private showing at th Royal Institute. Paul himself had reservations about hi

invention but was persuaded when it was put on a proper commercial basis; Harris and Paul took a fifty-fifty share of all the receipts at Olympia.

Even after his initial public success Paul still had little faith in his invention and began to sell cheap projector attachments for converting existing lanterns. He was selling parts to his future competitors. He also found himself inundated with requests from showmen for programmes of films to fit into their vaudeville shows. Before long Paul had twenty machines operating in provincial centres and was personally responsible for the running of eight nightly exhibitions in London.

The manager of another theatre in Leicester Square, the Alhambra, decided to give public performances of the 'new pictures' and Robert Paul was invited to begin a two-week season on 25th March 1896. For this new show he rechristened his invention the 'Animatograph'. It remained a success for four years. The public had bitten. In the meantime, Birt Acres had opened a show on a commercial basis in Piccadilly. The very first Royal performance took place in 1897 at Windsor Castle and Queen Victoria saw films made by the Lumière Brothers accompanied appropriately enough by the Empire Theatre Orchestra conducted by Leopold Wenzel. The royal seal of approval ensured the success of the new medium.

In the United States Edison's firm continued to perfect the Kinetoscope but it was the invention of Thomas Armat, an estate agent from Washington, that crystallised the idea of life-size projection. Edison's name was eventually use to promote the invention. On 4th April 1896 a priva exhibition was given in New York of 'Mr Edison's late invention', the 'Vitascope', an apparatus that projected th continuous Kinetoscope bands of film on to a large canva screen. On the night of 23rd April 1896 Edison's 'machin showing life' was demonstrated at Koster and Bial's Mus Hall in Herald Square, Broadway. According to the repo in the *New York Times* on the following day it was a singular exhilarating display. The programme of films included a umbrella dance 'by two precious blonde young persons o the variety stage', a burlesque boxing match, a comic allego called *The Monroe Doctrine* and 'a skirt dance by a ta blonde'. The short view of waves breaking on the shore a Dover (filmed by Birt Acres) momentarily filled the silk hatted audience with terror and their first reaction was t panic and run out or duck under the seats to avoid the spra

The showing of the Animatograph and the Lumiè films in 1896 established Leicester Square as the centre the British entertainment world, just as the showing of th Vitascope in Herald Square brought about the eventu acceptance of Broadway as the premier thoroughfare fo motion pictures in the United States. In both places som of the most expensive theatres in the world have since bee erected to show motion films.

The Empire Music Hall, Leicester Square, and its riva the old Alhambra, were the first long-term homes of ani mated pictures in England and it was from these variet

theatres that many of the basic ideas for the larger picture theatres a decade later emerged. Both theatres were noted for their spacious accommodation in the form of lounges, promenade spaces and ample foyers. The Empire, before it was replaced during the First World War, held about eight hundred people. The Alhambra, built in 1852 in the Moorish style, was converted to full cinema use in 1929 and later replaced by Oscar Deutsch's coal black Odeon in 1936.

Opposite **The Empire as a cinema**
Below **A contemporary engraving of the Empire**

The dissemination of films to a nation-wide publi brought its own problems, and experiments were made wit many novel ways of presentation. Thomas L Tally ha opened his picture parlour in 1897 in Los Angeles and th offered patrons the choice of Edison's peep-show Kinc toscope, the Mutoscope, an ear-tube phonograph or a com pletely blacked-out projection salon in which pictures coul be viewed on a screen. In 1902 Tally opened his first 'Electri Theatre' in Los Angeles with a continuous show 'especiall for ladies and children' from 7.30 to 10.30 each evenin The cinema thus made its debut as an independent an permanent entertainment in the United States.

The next important step forward in the presentation c motion pictures depended on two dissimilar aspects: firstl the development of the story film and secondly the intro duction in America of the 'Nickelodeon'. The Nickelodeo was simply a long narrow room with a rear stage, as often i not converted from an existing shop. By 1905 there we hundreds of little arcade theatres in the United State many of which had been used for Kinetoscope type ente tainment, and these also were converted to the new use projected pictures. A simple screen was erected, a curta was fixed between the audience and the front of the stag an area was usually reserved for a piano or small orchest in front of the curtain and the advertisement notices we erected on the front of the building. With closely pack wooden seats—or even benches—it was a poor prototy for the picture play-house of the next decade. The pr jection equipment, at that time occasionally powered petrol motors, was a dangerous element and although some examples it was placed in an isolated position abo the entrance more often it was just situated in the body the hall.

With the Nickelodeon the 'screen theatre' had rea arrived. Its inception was due to the business drive of tv men, Harry Davis and John P Harris, who opened th first establishment in a vacant store building in McKeespo Pittsburgh, Pennsylvania, in 1905. The first presentati was Edwin S Porter's one-reeler *The Great Train Robber* which had previously been billed as the 'photoplay se sation of 1903'. According to Ramsaye, business in t Nickelodeon (five cents and a Greek theatre) grew pr digiously and Harris and Davis were soon making a pro of nearly a thousand dollars a week and had extended t opening hours from 8.00 a.m. to midnight. The film bu

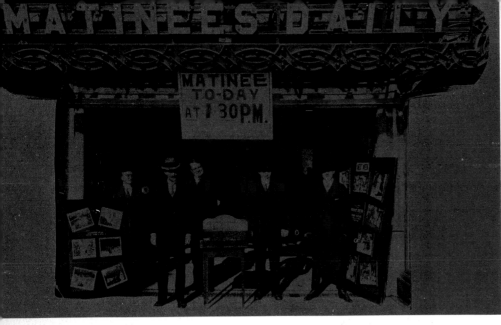

Left **A converted shop picture house**

Below left **One of the earliest London shop picture houses in Tottenham Court Road. Destroyed in 1929**

Below **An early picture of a converted picture house at Hammersmith Broadway c 1910**

Opposite **A typical American Nickelodeon and the Warner Brothers first movie house The Cascade at Newcastle, Pennsylvania, 1905**

Birmingham's West End, one of
the earliest entertainment
buildings built in England which
was converted to cinematograph
use at the turn of the century

e vast interior of the West End.
t, as one might imagine, a
inting by James Ensor

ness was gaining momentum. Within a short time nickelodeons could be counted in their thousands throughout the country. Pittsburgh had nearly a hundred of them within the year and New York succumbed to the 'Nickel Madness' with—and it was a journalistic estimate—three hundred gaudy examples by 1907. The businessmen close to the entertainment world immediately saw the opportunity of making a quick fortune and to many unscrupulous promoters a few seats, a second-hand projector and a screen were all that were needed to get under way if suitable vacant premises could be found. A narrow shop with a long interior was ideal.

As often as not the ordinary shop business was carried on in the front part of the premises and, if proper provision had not been made for obscuring the daylight, every time a customer came into the shop none of the audience behind could see the picture. In other cases the shop owner would subdivide his existing premises and graft in a movie hall. King Vidor in his autobiography *A Tree is a Tree* gives a graphic account of a typical conversion, the first movie picture house in Galveston, Texas, at Claude Brick's Music Store:

'When motion pictures came along, Claude pushed all of his pianos, drums and fiddles to the front of the store and built a thin wall across the centre. In this partition he constructed a box-office window and two openings, one marked "Entrance" and the other "Exit".'

This simple process of conversion was followed all over the United States and began spreading all over Britain a the Continent too. In England the nickelodeon was call a 'penny gaff', a name obviously derived from the itin ant show. With few restrictions on planning at that ti any old spacious building could be adapted to cinemat graphic use, especially if it held a prominent position ir busy street.

When skating rinks began to lose favour in the pub eye towards the end of the decade these were taken over promoters and used as cinemas. Many of them provid auditoria of substantial size, with a flat uninterrupted floc The Pavilion, Town End, Barnsley, was a typical skati rink conversion and opened as a cinema in 1911. Oth popular buildings for conversion in the North of Engla were the Mechanics' Institutes that had grown up as educ tional establishments in the nineteenth century, as well odd buildings like toffee factories and foundries. The St Picture Theatre at Huddersfield still had the old found under the auditorium floor when it was converted in 191 and the old tall foundry chimney remained as an inco gruous reminder of the building's former use.

The first decade of the new century had seen the progre of the film as a popular form of entertainment and whe buildings became directly designed to suit the new mediu fundamental changes took place. By 1910 the silent accompanied film had turned America and England in nations of cinema-goers whose preferences were similar b by no means identical.

3B

The itinerant
show

Opposite, top **Fairground shows.
Madamoiselle Lubina's varied
show which included short
films and live entertainment**
Below **Walter Hagger was a well
known showman who owned a
number of temporary booths.
This picture shows the front—
with the organ to the left and
the traction engine to the right—
of his 'Royal Electric' Bioscope**

Even before the promoters began their search for permanent buildings for the new medium the fairground structures of the showmen offered a temporary home. The travelling shows were on the move soon after the first exhibition of animated pictures in 1896. Having already warmed to the innovation of the peep-show and seen its popularity grow rapidly with audiences at fairs and shows throughout the country the showmen quickly caught on to the novelty of projecting films to a seated audience in a temporary structure. They bought up the commercial films that were being sold by the yard, purchased the necessary projection equipment and screens, created their show booths and inadvertently pioneered a trade.

The itinerant shows were an important feature of the pre-First World War movie industry. In fact it has been said that the industry would have failed without them. They bridged the gap between the ciné-variety shows, which had a short life in the old Music Halls, and the fixed show. The permanent show was introduced only towards the end of the first decade of this century after the new industry had gained a firm foothold and a respectability with the general public. The travelling show disappeared soon after the outbreak of the First World War.

A large share of the honours for pioneering film throughout the world must be given to the show-people who invested very large sums of money in their booths and in many cases produced their own films for exclusive showing. They were not of the same breed as the cinema operators who, out for a quick penny, offered performances in ch[e] run-down shop premises or rented halls.

Some of the travelling shows were magnificently elab[or]ate structures, many of them far more expensive to run th[an] the later permanent examples. Indeed, according to [the] memory of patrons who visited these shows, they w[ere] more loved and appreciated by owners and customers th[an] the first picture palaces. They had their own traditio[nal] venues, their own competitive 'gimmicks', and times [of] opening that suited everyone (usually from 10 a.m. [to] midnight). From an architectural point of view they a[lso] had a distinctive temporary structure, built both for fu[nc]tional efficiency and to give a strong visual impression.

Few records of these early shows were kept and wh[at] recollections there are seem to be stored in the minds [of] the people who saw them. Scanty reference is made to t[he] displays of 'living pictures', 'Bioscope Shows' and 'cinem[a]tograph exhibitions' in the local papers of the time and on[ly] a hazy picture emerges of what the shows were really li[ke.] The *Hull News* in October 1898 referred to 'a new form [of] public entertainment' in a description of the exhibits at t[he] Hull Fair in that year: 'waxworks, ghost shows and troup[es] of performing insects have given way to exhibitions of mo[re] or less scientific interest. Animated photographs of differe[nt] names, and shows, the fundamental principle of which [is] electricity, are now *de rigeur*. Peep shows have been su[p]planted by phonographs!' Randall Williams brought h[is] Bioscope to the fair with 'some new and up-to-date scene[s]

38

The crowd around
Thurston's Fairground show,
St Giles Fair, Oxford, 1905

Opposite **A Dutch travelling show,
c 1909, and below, the fantastic
Art Nouveau inspired façade of
Jean Desmet's Bioscope that
travelled throughout the Low
Countries under the title of 'The
Imperial Bio'**

Below **A busker outside the Pathe
Brothers' travelling show, 1906**

In an article by Edgar Appleton, again in a Hull pa[...]
the *Daily Mail* (1953), a fascinating glimpse of the e[...]
productions shown at the fairs is given: 'The first mov[...]
picture I saw, was at Hull Fair. This must have been ab[...]
the time of the Boer War. The film was called "Saving [...]
Despatches" and must have been made on Ilkley M[...]
for the vegetation was decidely non-tropical. There w[...]
no captions, but we were kept aware of what was going [...]
by a *raconteur* who, on occasion, was pretty well spru[...]
Raynor's Penny Show, a portable unit—but not strictl[...]
fairground show—that was situated on sites in Nottingh[...]
at the turn of the century, also showed pictures of the B[...]
War, but this time they were combined with variety tur[...]

In Nottingham the Goose Fair was the main venue for
travelling shows and in 1897 two impressive marquee[...]
Collins's Living Pictures and Captain T Payne's Elect[...]
Bioscope—attracted vast crowds to see such items [...]
'Little Jim—the collier's child' and 'Wet Paint—benc[...]
in the park'. Admission for these shows was twopence [...]
adults and a penny for children.

Captain Payne declared that the Electric Bioscope offer[...]
films with 'steadiness and no flickering' but once inside t[...]
patron found the claim distressingly inaccurate as the fo[...]
minute films flickered and vibrated their way across t[...]
muslin screen. As well as the large-scale shows at t[...]
Goose Fair other competitors exhibited under the nam[...]
of the Vitagraph, Proctor's Show, President Kem[...]
Theatre, Caddick's American Theatre and Wall's Gh[...]
Show or Phantascope.

One of the earliest of the travelling shows was built [...]
Savage's of Kings Lynn in 1897. It was a canvas-cover[...]
arena sixty feet by forty feet with a boarded floor and [...]
elaborately carved front. It could seat forty customers [...]
folding seats and could also cater for a prestige client[...]
with twelve plush front-row seats with arms. The relative[...]
bare interior had a small stage. The paybox and front we[...]
gilded and decorated with life-size carved statues and t[...]
whole frontage was lit at night by giant electric lamp[...]
Added to this attraction was the large steam organ th[...]
boomed out its tune at the start of each performance.

Arthur Fay's booklet *Bioscope Shows and their Engi[...]
gives an interesting account of the sort of show that took [...]
the road. Fay, who had first-hand experience of the trave[...]
ling shows, recalls the stories about the weather and tran[...]
portation hazards that beset the showmen and the incredib[...]

Dutch travelling show
Carlos Riozzi's Bioscope
ed Dutch travelling show
newer ideas for advertising
c 1912

and Below Two English
ling shows

THE UNC... ...OLA.

TO-DAY TO BE SEEN HERE ONLY.
CRIPPEN AND LE'NEVE.
THE LATEST SENSATION.

HULL FAIR 34

A booth at Hull Fair

amount of care and money that went into the shows. He also gives some account of the reaction of the audience to the various shows up and down the country. He describes the visual fascination the travelling shows had for the public and the wonderful names they had: Mrs Weir's Electric Chronograph Empire, Taylor's Coliseum, Mrs Holland's Palace of Light, Collins's Wonderland and Wadbrook's Royal Electrograph were typical titles. Each one had its own technique of presentation, and nearly all exploited, far earlier than did the cinema architect, the use of external electric signs and flood-lighting effects. In fact these shows were small electric pavilions that drew their audiences around their light source, like moths around a flame.

Inside they were dark. Perhaps this more than anyth... else earned them the contempt of those puritanical peo... who felt that the showmen were the devil's disciples ... used their palaces of light and darkness to seduce the yo... and weak-willed from the path of goodness. This is a bo... that has followed the industry throughout its history.

The Bioscope shows competed with each other in g... deur and decoration. The owner's chief pride was in ... front, usually a massive ornamentally carved and gil... structural wall lit either by floods or by a multitude of si... light sources.

Two of the finest shows that toured England were ... Holland's Palace of Light and Pat Collins's Wonderla...

46

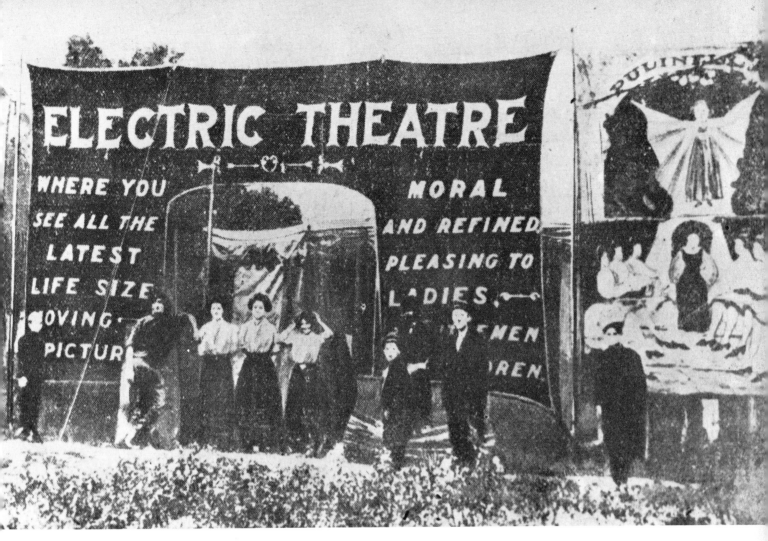

Electric Theatre, a canvas
ted fairground show

Palace of Light was an enormous structure accommo-
ng about 1,000 people, with 600 seats and room for 400
ding in a gallery. The internal finishes were lavish, with
seats upholstered in green figured cloth and groups of
anese style lamp-shades hanging from the roof, Fay
s that 'the general lighting system of the interior was
ost identical to that of many other travelling Cinemas
consisted of four golden arc lamps on the central ridge
two at the extreme end of the booth in close proximity
he moving picture medium'. The proscenium itself was
ved and gilded in a similar manner to the front.
ome idea of the scale of the show places and the trans-
tation difficulties encountered can be deduced from the

Palace of Light, which required a 26 foot truck to carry
the proscenium alone.

In 1912 Mrs Holland's Palace caught fire in Anglesey
and within twenty minutes nothing was left but ashes.
Collins's Wonderland appeared at the Mammoth Fun City
at Olympia in 1907 before going on tour. It played to
packed houses. A contemporary magazine described it as
the finest show with the finest exterior in England. Its
elaborate gilt façade was lit by fourteen powerful arc-lamps
and 5,000 multi-coloured electric lamps set into the carved
wooden ornament. A switching-on ceremony took place
every evening drawing vast crowds for what Collins called
an 'electric firework display'. The power for these lights

came from the big road traction engine that usually stood to one side of the symmetrically placed paybox and entrance steps. On the platform at the other side, except where it was used for dancing girls, stood the ornamental 'paper' organ.

Not all the booths were as ambitious as the two just described. Indeed, as with many cinema buildings some twenty years later, little thought was given to the comfort of the customer or the quality of the picture. Most of the travelling shows had projectors worked by hand and the result was usually chaotic. The highly inflammable film fell off the single spool (no take-up spool was provided) into a basket or bucket underneath the machine. Not noted for clarity of definition in the first place the early films suffered from the inexperience of the operator as well as

**A poster for the first travelling
show of the Albert-Frères, 1899**

his temperament. A further annoyance found in a b[a]run show was the owner's desire to get through each [per]formance (usually 30–40 minutes) as soon as possible allow the next audience in. But ironically this 'rushing' often frustrated by the film breaking or tangling an[d] some cases by the whole projection equipment expirin[g] bursting into flames. The exhibition of films under t[he] circumstances became a very vocal community act, [with] the audience joining in with its jeers and comments and operator adding his expletives.

The fairground show soon had other competitors, als[o] a temporary and mobile character. The mobile pic[ture] threatre took a number of forms, from the single van t[o] which projected film from its roof on to an outdoor sc[reen] positioned in a public square, to the idiosyncratic entert[ain]ment provided at the beginning of the century by Ge[orge] Hale in his simulated motion vehicles. Hale's 'Tours' these exhibitions were called, had been introduced at St. Louis Louisiana Purchase Exposition in 1904. Hal[e] former chief fire officer to Kansas City, was responsible organising a display of his famous firefighters at the Ex[po]sition. In an unofficial capacity he also introduced his 'To[urs] and Scenes of the World' from which he eventually amas[sed] a fortune. This attraction was a new kind of filmed illus[ion]

It was a simple enough idea: travel films were exhib[ited] in a structure resembling a railway coach which was roc[ked] from side to side (by unseen attendants) simulating [the] motion of a train. The lights were switched off and [the] projector flashed pictures on to a screen—cleverly [dis]guised as a window at the front of the coach—and [the] spectator was off on a journey through the Swiss Alp[s or] Yellowstone Park. To complete the illusion a ticket colle[ctor] —in suitable uniform—stood at the entrance to the 'co[ach] to clip tickets and every now and then to wave his fla[g or] blow a whistle. After the success at the Fair, Hale s[old] facsimiles of his show all over America, and soon tiny do[wn] town theatres as well as Coney Island were packing the[m in] to see the Tours.

In 1906 Hale brought his novelty to England. [The] audience was charged sixpence per head and various v[er]sions of the show were to be seen in the main cities of [the] country. The Oxford Street and Nottingham Hales To[urs] survived until 1912 when they were superseded by the m[ore] sophisticated story films that were being shown in the m[ore] comfortable surroundings of the permanent cinema.

**Cinema buildings
in Britain before
the first world war**

It was not until after the middle of the first decade of this century that new buildings designed for the exclusive exhibition of motion pictures began to appear.

As early as 1897 film distributing companies were set up in England—in most cases as offshoots of American concerns—and these multiplied considerably once promoters saw film as a potential trade rather than simply a showman's novelty. In 1904 A C Bromhead—who had launched the Gaumont Company in England with T A Welch in 1898—opened the first of his 'Daily Bioscope' theatres for exclusive cinematograph use in Bishopsgate Street, London. Bromhead's venture was followed by other small 'Electric Palaces' and 'Bioscope Theatres', all of which were in fact slightly refined versions of the penny gaffs (old shops with new fronts). Their programmes consisted mainly of topical news items interspersed with short situation comedies.

These slightly more sophisticated structures were the exception rather than the rule during the early years and generally the pattern of exhibiting pictures at fairgrounds, music halls, town halls and vacant buildings continued. Of these the town hall show grew in popularity very quickly and often, due to public demand, the showmen responsible for hiring the halls extended their season indefinitely. It was not a very adequate arrangement and the hired public hall soon lost favour with the new promoters who turned their attention back to the legitimate theatre and the music hall, not to fill in an odd act here and there but to convert the whole building to an all-picture house. The Theatre Royal,

Attercliffe, Sheffield, opened for permanent cinematogr[a] performances in 1904 with accommodation for 950 peo[ple] Another well-known example of this type of conversion [was] the Balham Empire which re-opened its doors in 190[7] one of the first London theatres devoted exclusively to fil[m].

The Empire was operated by the British Cinema C[om]pany and showed pictures by the Pathé Frères. The tw[o] hour programme set a precedent for the all-picture sho[w] with twice-nightly performances, matinees Wednesday [and] Saturday, and music supplied by an orchestra. The o[ne] major difference between this and shows later on—wh[en] the feature film came into popularity—was the numbe[r of] separate films shown—fourteen 'scenes' was the aver[age] length of programme in 1907.

According to Rachel Low, in her book *The History [of] British Film*, the Islington Empire and the New Thea[tre] St Martins Lane, soon followed the Empire's example [in] showing pictures. Others, like the well-known Birkenh[ead] Music Hall, The Argyle, alternated for a time with picture shows in some weeks and variety shows in othe[rs].

This conventional type of theatre still did not fulfil [the] needs of the new medium and problems arose that could [not] be overcome without considerable alterations to the str[uc]ture and seating arrangements of the existing buildin[g]. Better buildings, tailored to the planning and visual [re]quirements of film projection, were needed. The first cr[ude] attempts to provide this began around 1907. A building t[hat] can actually be called the first cinema—designed exclusiv[ely]

osite **Joshua Duckworth and
Central Hall, Colne, Lancs,
1**. The old Central Hall, now
t of an engineering works is
sidered to be probably the
t building built in England
usively for showing movies
t **A programme title page and
ter for The Gem, Faversham,
4**

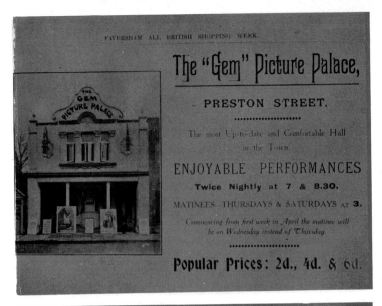

d especially for film shows—is difficult to trace. Most
ely it was the Central Hall, Colne, built for Joshua
uckworth in 1907. The original form of this building can
ll be seen although it now forms part of the central works
the Cleveland Engineering Company. Duckworth was
ll known as a showman and notices of his 'high class'
ows are to be found in the early editions of the *Kinemato-
iph and Lantern Weekly*.

This magazine, which changed its title from *The Optical
intern and Kinematograph Journal* in 1907, still serves the
n industry under its popular name of *Kine Weekly*. From
e 1907 edition of *Kine* some idea of the state of the film
ide at that time can be deduced. It had already been con-
lidated in 1906 in an agreement signed by the men of
licker Alley' (which was Cecil Court off London's
naring Cross Road).

'All picture shows' were on the increase, the *Kine* re-
orted in 1907, and the first public exhibition of talking
ctures through the 'illusion of life' technique (not to be
nfused with the later Talkies) was given at the London
ippodrome. On the cover of the first edition of 16th May
107 an advertisement appeared for Pathé Frères (who
ere not incidentally signatories to the 1906 document)
aiming that they were the largest film manufacturers in
e world with an actual daily output of 70,000 yards. No
oubt this was a justification for their further claim that they
ere 'pioneers of the 4d. per foot'.

Following on Duckworth's pioneering work in establish-

ing the premier English palace in the small Lancash
industrial town of Colne, the main provincial towns led
way in providing new cinemas. Birmingham was well ah
but Manchester by 1913 had more cinemas per head
population than any other city in the country. In the no
west, according to the *Kine Year Book 1913*, Manchester l
111 cinemas, Liverpool 22, Birkenhead 11, Stockport 9
Bolton 8. The actual number of cinemas in London at t
time was, of course, much higher—the LCC had gran
200 licences for cinematograph theatres by 1910—but t
were spread over an area with a far greater population

With the new buildings came a new image. This ima
which became the preoccupation of promoters in the th
years after 1908, was succinctly described by Rachel L
'More and more effort was spent in impressing
audience with comfort and elegance, and providing
pictures worthy of better-class audiences. Red plush a
marble, ferns in brass pots and plenty of electric light w
guaranteed to give that "air of cosy refinement" which v
wistfully sought by a trade anxious to disclaim its low bir
The foyer must have bevelled mirrors if it was to acqu
the prized *bon ton* which would make it a really "high-cl
rendezvous". Refinements like shaded lights, uniform
young (sometimes very young) attendants instead of the
barker, and "tasteful plaster mouldings" to adorn
front of the up-to-date pretty picture palace became a cu
The theatres varied in size from a couple of hundred se
to 1,000 or even 2,000, but size and splendour were of l

The old Brinksway Pictorium, Stockport, c 1912. Another early building designed as a small picture house which now serves other uses

importance than good taste, elegance, and the preoccupation with daintiness.'

The precious vocabulary the promoters drew on, as Rachel Low goes on to say, reflected the same search for class; the Globe, Bijou Palace, Gem, Pictorium, Imperial, Empire and Jewel were some of the more favourite names.

It was the claim of picture-house owners and designers in this period that cinema auditoria needed more decoration and ornament than those of ordinary theatres, 'the better to satisfy a more general taste'.

The stage, it was felt, was indispensable in a picture house because of the need for space for intermission acts, for giving a shadow bow effect around the screen and to add depth to the picture itself. The common practice of showing films in complete darkness was also questioned by designers and promoters and some experiments took place with daylight and artificial light projection. Immediately after the First World War most picture houses used soft amber or rose-tinted lamps for low-level illumination (known as 'morality lighting') throughout performances. The obsessive desire for respectability by cinema owners meant that they no longer hired benches from the local caterer or undertaker: upholstered tipping seats replaced them in the auditorium and drawing-room furniture appeared in the foyer.

The desire for better buildings for the movies was not entirely fortuitous. It was very largely conditioned by the demands for safety and licensing outlined in the Cinematograph Act, 1909, which became operative on 1st January 1910. This Act had become necessary because of the inflammable nature of the films used at the time which had a cellulose-nitrate base and which when old or in a state of decomposition often ignited and burned with an explosive force. This type of film created a fire hazard when stored under unsatisfactory conditions and was the cause of a number of well publicized cinema blazes. The general public had begun to fear for their lives every time they entered a picture house.

The immediate effect of the Act was to force cinema owners to spend more on their buildings and it was soon realised that a laissez-faire attitude was no longer valid. The owners had done things their own way for nearly thirty years. Even the fairground show did not escape the provisions of the Act and reference was made to the showing of pictures in 'booth, tent or structure'. The Act laid down rules that made the provision of a separate fire-resisting projection booth obligatory. The entrance door to the booth had to be close-fitting and constructed of fire-proof material. The projection ports were to be limited in size and there had to be not more than two of these for each machine. An automatically controlled screen had to be fitted inside and outside the enclosure so that any fire could be confined within the area in which it broke out. The safety measures to be observed in the auditorium affected the number and widths of entrance doors and free unobstructed access to them. The Act also insisted on the provision of fire appliances—a damp blanket, two buckets

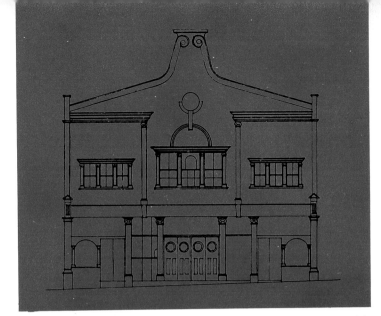

front elevation of the
...fair, Tottenham, c 1912

ter and a bucket of dry sand. Toilet facilities had to be ...vided for staff and stage artistes as well as for the paying ...blic. All cinemas in Britain in this early period of the ...dustry were built with permanence in mind, with a solid ...d 'impressive' front. The promoters, it seems, constantly ...d one eye fixed on American practice. However, it is ...eresting to note that as early as 1916 one American ...chitect, Edwin O Sachs, considered a cinema building to ...ve only a limited life of 18 years although his reasons for ...s belief are obscure.

How long the early examples have lasted can be judged by ...ring the central and southern suburbs of London. The ...oscope (now the Biograph) still exists in Victoria, al- ...ough recently it has been completely ruined externally by ...insensitive 'face-lift'. This building was converted from ...ow of shops in about 1905 by an American promoter, ...eorge Washington Grant. Internally it is decorated in what ...eoffrey Fletcher has graphically described as 'ham-fisted ...roque'. Later London examples followed this prototype, ...d the pseudo-Classicism proliferated on the outside. ...sentially the cinemas in the period 1910–1914 were ...corated fronts with corrugated-iron halls behind. The ...ain front had little or nothing in common with the sides ...d rear of the same building—in fact, in many of the early ...lls it is difficult to believe that all the parts on a site belong ... the same structure. This pattern of development no ...ubt derived directly from the ornamental treatment of ...e fairground 'fronts'. The Walpole Picture Theatre,

Ealing (1912), was typical of this sort of treatment but with high class 'artistic' details in addition, while at Brixton Hill a cinema built in about 1910 (now a Camping Centre) has a front that has clearly been stuck on to a rectangular hall.

The debased Classical detailing common to picture houses travelled far and wide, and the Pavilion, Rundle Street, Adelaide (1912), was a significant version, complete with Empire-style decoration. Internally the 'Pav' was a big hollow barn with a high ceiling and no balcony, similar to many English examples.

The Globe, Putney (c. 1910), still retains its original form as a simple, rectangular, single-floor structure spanned by a reinforced concrete roof. The entrances on either side of the centrally positioned paybox give access directly into the auditorium from the pavement. Externally the Globe has the two small moorish openwork domes that were also a feature of many early cinemas, poised rather precariously on either side of the main façade.

In the large provincial cities in England cinema buildings were increased in size by 1911. The Picture House, Oxford Street, Manchester (now the New Oxford, although parts of the old façade still remain), was opened in 1911 and was by any standard a fine and efficient building. A barrel-vaulted structure, it accommodated 1,000 patrons in a spacious stalls area—with centre and side aisles—and on a balcony that was reached by a large staircase rising from the oak panelled vestibule. It was a mature building of its type

WALPOLE PICTURE THEATRE

& CONTRACTORS.
OVIS

t 10.

THE
WALPOLE
PICTURE THEATRE
BOND ST EALING

BOOKS OF TICKETS
AT THE BOX OFFICE

OPENING
MONDAY,
JULY 29TH
AT 3 O'CLOCK

SEATING CAPACITY
1,600
CONTINUOUS PERFORMANCE

THE
WALPOLE
PICTURE THEATRE
BOND ST EALING

OPENING
MONDAY,
JULY 29TH
AT 3 O'CLOCK

SEATING CAPACITY
1,600
CONTINUOUS PERFORMANCE

BOOKS OF TICKETS
AT THE BOX OFFICE

show front and interior of
Walpole Picture Theatre,
ng, 1912

Right The projection room in the
Star Theatre, Adelaide, Australia,
1912, and, below, the exterior of
the Pavilion Picture Theatre (now
the Rex), Adelaide of the same
date

Below The 'Islamic' exterior of
The Globe, Putney, c 1910

The Salford Cinema (Rex) about 1912

An early cinema on Brixton (c 1910) that is now used as a [shopp]ing centre

[wit]h an auditorium luxuriously decorated with hanging [tap]estries, an 'entirely fireproof Lantern Room' separated [fro]m the public areas, a screen recessed and draped with [blac]k velvet, and a ventilation system (a modification of [the] 'Plenum' type) that gave ten air changes per hour. [Thi]s building was erected for Provincial Cinematograph [The]atres Ltd and was claimed at the time to be no more [effi]cient and attractive than those opened or in the course [of e]rection by that company in Bristol, Birmingham, Leeds, [Lei]cester, Nottingham, Portsmouth, Belfast, Dublin, [Edi]nburgh and Glasgow.

[M]anchester had a unique place in England's early cinema [bui]lding history. Today, many of these early cinema build-[ing]s can still be seen more or less in their original state. [So]me still show films, others have changed to 'bingo' or [com]mercial use. Although the old Bijou Electric at Hulme [and] the Imperial Palace at Moston have vanished, the [Gr]osvenor, All Saints, the Salford (Rex) cinema (now a store [ho]use), the Deansgate Picture Hall (now the Cinephone) and [the] Oxford Street Picture House mentioned previously still [rem]ain. The Grosvenor, All Saints, built in 1912, is a per-[fec]t surviving example of the pre-war picture house, with [cre]am and green faience tiled elevations on two streets, a [sma]ll copper dome over the corner entrance and an interior [tha]t is more like an Edwardian music hall than a cinema.

[T]he first cinema to open in the centre of Glasgow was [the] Electric Theatre. Built in 1909 it became the social [M]ecca' of the cinema-going public. This picture theatre—

The 'artistic' splendour of the provincial cinema is shown here with a Birmingham example from the years before the First World War

Below The entrance foyer and a detail of the proscenium

Opposite The auditorium and screen

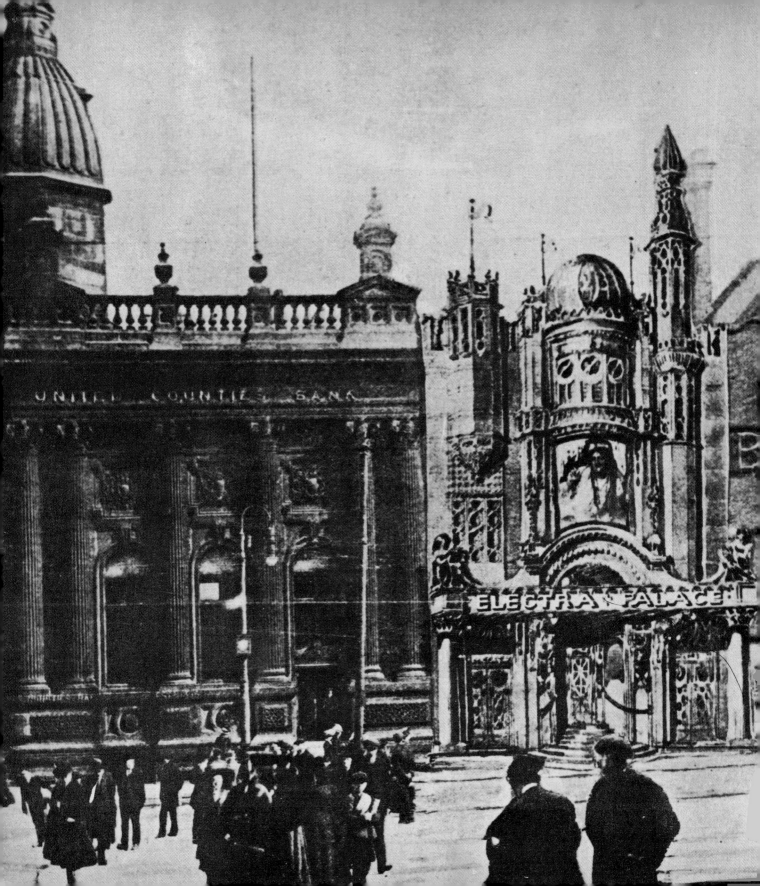

its Palm Court Tea Rooms equipped with fountains, fish pool and cages of singing birds—was the place in gow where the working class mum and her daughter d with the 'fine-folk'. Pictures, it seems, at this early had transcended those distinctions of class that had perpetuated by the legitimate theatre.

he Electric Theatre in Kensington, opened in 1909, laid claim to the fact that it was patronized by the *élite*, y of whom came in 'motor cars and carriages'. The inual clamour by the promoters for class soon brought it a confusion of aims.

his was quickly overshadowed by the erection of erous new cinemas in towns where the population— icularly in the central areas—was largely working-class. rwards, in the late 'twenties and early 'thirties, it was olicy of more than one film company to site their more ptuous buildings deliberately in the poorest areas. This not a philanthropic gesture but one firmly based on the on that the illusions created by films gave the working- s cinema-goer the vicarious pleasure he desired.

s early as 1910 the Sheffield and District Cinematograph atre Company was formed for the purpose of 'erecting equipping in the busiest and most thickly populated s of the City and District, Cinematograph Theatres on o-date lines similar to those so successfully established ondon and large Provincial Towns'. The capital amount led by the new company was £50,000. With a guaranteed ulation of half a million in the region to draw on, the ess of the venture, it was felt, would be inevitable. The pany's immediate plan was to build an Electra Palace land that had been acquired early in 1910 in Fitzalan are. In 1912 the Electra, designed by Hickton and mer of Birmingham, opened with accommodation for patrons. It was slightly smaller than its competitor the on Street Picture Palace that had opened its doors in o. These two cinemas in Sheffield were soon followed another, the more ambitious Unity Picture Palace, gsett Road, opened in 1913 and designed by Gibbs, ckton and Teather. The Unity Picture house was cted at a cost of £6,000 and accommodated 750 people he saloon floor and about 250 in the balcony. The stage he rear of the screen was originally intended for variety or public meetings, and dressing rooms for stage shows e provided. The building was heated by hot-water ators and ventilated by two electric extractor fans in

The Palace, Sheffield, 1910

Opposite **A preliminary drawing for the Electra Palace, Sheffield. It was eventually completed, with a different frontage, in 1912**

63

1913

PALACE ✿ CINEMA

& SONS
OUTFITTERS

Youths'
Suits
from
10/6

2/6 The IMPERIAL 2/6
TURKISH BATHS
Russell Square
For FINEST in WORLD
LADIES & GENTLEMEN
Electric Light Baths
Fix & Vichy Douches
Medicated Baths
Vibro & Electric Massage
Electro Therapeutic Treatment
Culture

osite **The front of the Palace**
ema, Kentish Town, 1913

ve **The interior of the Palace**

the ceiling and inlets behind the radiators. The traditional theatre-like exterior was faced with pressed brick and Huddersfield stone dressings and the roof was covered with grey asbestos tiling.

Many of these early Sheffield picture houses, like others in northern towns, had billiard halls or restaurants attached. Written into the licence clauses was also the provision that the building could be adapted to some other form of entertainment use such as a skating rink or a public hall. This hesitant feeling about the lasting popularity of films was also reflected in the precaution some promoters took of re-introducing variety turns in their bills. This time the acts took place in buildings designed for cinema performances! Another inducement to get the paying public in and to give more interest to a show was the employment of a narrator, who introduced the silent films and related the plot as the story unfolded.

Another real but less practical uncertainty was to be found in the constant debates that took place in the press at the times about the instructional and educative value of films. Sub-titles on American films were particularly suspect as it was thought they would ruin the purity of the English language, and the effects of wicked foreign films on children caused many local authorities to preclude their admittance.

The new medium's supposed limitations from an artistic point of view were voiced by many critics and the following is an extract from a criticism by John Palmer written in 1913:

'The picture palace has tapped a vast public looking cheap amusement. It threatens to slay utterly the trave show, nigger minstrels, the panorama, and the circu has won a permanent place for itself as an item of vaudev But we shall in a few years hear little of its competition the theatre. Nor will those stuffy and stupefying pic palaces be able for long to maintain themselves in t hundred thousands. The limitations of this form of en tainment, already eked out in the larger palaces with mu hall varieties, will soon appear, and the interest even of threepenny public be exhausted.'

How wrong Palmer was. There certainly was a tempo slump in attendances in 1914 but this was caused by exacerbating effects of an unpredictable Amusement and rising costs of programmes as well as by the outbi of war. It was not the result of any lack of interest fi patrons. Paradoxically, this period was helpful to the inc try because it cleared the country of the temporary s and the unprofitable small buildings. A conservative mate puts the number of cinemas successfully operatin 1914 as 3,500. By 1918 seven or eight hundred of these closed. During the war years the film industry in Bri consolidated its position in terms of its stock of buildi When building activity was resumed after the war the l rectangular hall with a minimum of pre-auditorium sp was replaced by the larger cinema that seated audience thousands instead of hundreds and which copied Ameri ideas on size, planning and decoration.

interior and exterior of The
estic Picturedrome,
tenham Court Road, 1912

ow **A page from the daily**
eipt book of the Scala Theatre,
ttingham, the day after
land entered the First World

leaf **The solid façade of**
Picture House, Portsmouth,
5

SCALA THEATRE, NOTTINGHAM

Summary of Daily Receipts.

For ...Wednes...day, the ...5th... day of ~~July~~ Aug. 1914

	Admit- tances.				TOTAL.		Total for corresponding day of previous year.	
STALLS	299	4	8	7				
CIRCLE	202	4	17	4				
PIT	165	3	2	9				
	146	1	4	4				
			13	13	0	14	7	8
PROGRAMMES								
Cigarettes & Cigars			2	2				
SWEETS			7	9				
MINERALS								
TEAS								
			9	11	9	11	13	6
TOTAL			14	2	11	18	1	2

Weather: Fine

Remarks: War fever in Nottingham. Everybody outside awaiting news.

Frederic D Smith   Manager.

The American origins
of movie palace
architecture

The growth of picture houses in America in the period 1910–20 was phenomenal. 'Movie madness' pervaded society and by the middle of the decade it has been estimated that 25,000 picture theatres were in use and the average daily attendance was in the region of six million people.

Many of the big old theatre buildings in the more important towns were rapidly converted into cinema use with films becoming an important part of the vaudeville programme. It was a process which, like the shop shows and Nickelodeons of the previous decade, required little expense and hardly any additional work. A simple screen was erected, often of plain muslin on a wooden or iron frame, and an area sealed off for projection equipment. When the stage was in use for vaudeville acts the screen was merely lifted into the fly tower or carefully rolled and stored at the back behind the flats. In these early days of the American movie industry, buildings designed exclusively as cinemas were still rare, and throughout the country the supporting vaudeville acts were generally considered to be of more importance. This feeling was to last right through to the golden days of the movie palace when even the most extravagent structures had full stage facilities and stage companies often numbering hundreds.

Those buildings that were devoted exclusively to film shows—small neighbourhood houses called 'Pictureplay Theatres'—were crude in comparison to the luxury theatre. In an attempt to make them more acceptable promoters began dressing the area immediately in front of the screen and introduced better materials for the screen itself. M Grecian or Italianate styles were in vogue for a perman setting around the screen, and arches, columns, perist and cornices were knocked up out of timber to provide appropriate effect. Amid the potted plants and the casional fountain, scenes were depicted on angled which were meant to emphasise the three-dimensio make-believe of the picture on the screen. Below the scr sat a group of orchestral players frantically trying to k time with the action of the silent films and filling in du the intervals with popular songs of the day.

To improve the quality of the picture on the scr owners resorted to the use of aluminium dust or powde glass to get a brilliance on the white painted muslin. T was superseded in some picture houses by the use of a g screen—with a gold or silver back—which forme reflective surface and thus gave a greater clarity to the p jected picture. Needless to say it also reflected any st light that got into the auditorium as well as the bald he of the orchestral players if it was wrongly positioned was soon found also that the sheer weight of the plate g and the effects of condensation did not make glass an ic screen material and buildings began to be constructed corporating a narrow apron stage with a screen formed of plaster of Paris on the rendered rear wall of the buildi

In the United States, laws relating to the design erection of picture theatres were established by S Authorities. These affected the detail design of the buildi

LESLIE
HOWARD
in
"PYGMALION"
by
BERNARD
SHAW
★ ★ ★ ★

STAR THEATRE

4 STAR THEATRE
BERNARD SHAW'S "PYGMALION" LESLIE HOWARD WENDY HILLER
PRODUCED BY GABRIEL PASCAL-DISNEY'S "SOCIETY DOG SHOW"

CONTINUOUS
FROM 2.30
"PYGMALION"

rrie

SALE

PYGMALION

Wilshire Nut Shop

POPCORN

The foyer of Loew's 175th Street
Picture Theatre, New York

A Buddha on the balcony of
Loew's 72nd Street Picture
Theatre

, as is customary with building regulations throughout
erica, they differed quite widely from state to state. For
mple, in New York State it was necessary for the designer
uild in fireproof material where the total seating capacity
eeded 100, while in Seattle it was only necessary to do so
e capacity exceeded 750. The State of Ohio required
all projection equipment should be hand-driven.
nsylvania did not allow balconies, but did require
chanical ventilation in the auditorium. Requirements
the width and number of exits, aisles and seat spacing
e in most cases similar throughout the country and
responded to those required by the Cinematograph
ulations in Britain.

After 1912, with the marked improvement in quality of
nt films, a new type of picture theatre emerged. Enter-
sing promoters envisaged a golden future for the movie
ustry and plans began for exclusive and expensive
ises in New York. The first major luxury picture theatre,
e Regent, was opened in 1913 on the corner of 116th
eet and Seventh Avenue. Designed by Thomas W Lamb,
cottish-born architect, it was the quintessence of movie
ace architecture. Unfortunately it failed to bring in the
ormous crowds the promoters dreamed of and soon the
ns were receiving the usual support from stage turns.
But within the year things changed. S L Rothafel (the
nk Lloyd Wright of the cinema world, commonly known
Roxy') had arrived in New York. Under manager Roxy's
idance the Regent became the showplace of Harlem.

After that it was the turn of Broadway. Roxy moved into
the newly-completed Strand Theatre on 47th Street to
a blaze of publicity in the spring of 1914. This was
Thomas Lamb's second spectacular movie house structure
and it was meant to be admired as a model of all future
Moving Picture Palaces. It did in fact inaugurate the new
era in American picture house design with 'gilt and marble
and deep pile rugs, crystal chandeliers hanging from the
ceiling and original art works on the walls, with luxurious
lounges and comfortable chairs, a thirty-piece symphony
orchestra . . . and a mighty Wurlitzer'. Against this background of superficial splendour Roxy thrilled the gaping
audiences with spectacular musical entertainment followed
by the main feature film. After the Strand, the Rialto
(formerly Hammerstein's Music Hall) and the new Rivoli,
both designed by Lamb, became the places in which Roxy
displayed his skill as the world's greatest showman. Roxy,
at once theatre manager, interior decorator, impresario and
his own publicity expert, succeeded where other men had
failed. He brought the movie palace to the people at prices
they could afford and with a decorative flourish that swept
them off their feet.

The whole story of Roxy's rise to fame and fortune is
told in Ben Hall's fine and amusing book, *The Best Remaining Seats*, and in this a good idea can be had of the changing
role the architect played in the design of the new sumptuous
movie palaces. Thomas W Lamb quickly established a
position for himself as the most sought-after picture theatre

designer in America. He was, as Ben Hall says, 'the dean of the *standard* (or 'hard-top') school and the first major architect to make his name in movie theatres'. Following on his heels were C Howard Crane of Detroit and John Eberson, the European-trained creator of the *atmospheric* interior.

The work of these three architects characterised the whole movement towards luxury and elegance in movie palace architecture. The treatment of the exteriors of the buildings was invariably in the Classical manner, often faced with terra-cotta blocks, simulating the work of the Masters of the Renaissance or facsimiles of parts of the Louvre, but the interiors were original works of art ranging from the preference Lamb had for Adam and Empire styling to the Pompeian and Grecian motifs used by Eberson.

At the beginning of the 'twenties duplicates of the great New York movie palaces were going up and huge capacity houses seating anything up to 5,000 were soon to be found in all the key cities of America. Lamb's Capitol, opened on Broadway in 1919, had clearly shown that nothing need be spared in the attempt to make the movie palace the most splendid type of building since the Renaissance. Murals, rock-crystal chandeliers, elaborate staircases, fine draperies, silver and gold leaf, mahogany panelling, all were part of the new affluent image used by the extravagant promoters to entice customers into the magic world of richness that was missing in their homes.

Lamb's output was prodigious and by 1921 he had responsible for the erection of over 300 theatres. His re tation had been enhanced by the tasteful way in which designed, with simple almost conventional theatre exte turned to movie use and with a touch of flamboyance and there. The Baroque-roguery of other designers see shamefully extravagant in comparison.

John Eberson's work provides a complete contrast to work of all other architects designing movie palace America. Eberson, trained in Vienna and Dresden, vented the 'stars and clouds' interior which relied on use of 'manufactured weather', ingenious lighting eff and stage set decoration. The 'atmospheric' was fir rooted in a conviction that visual gimcrackery is primary demand of the paying public and the more sp dour and glitter that can be brought together to ins an audience the better they will respond. Eberson's teriors were complete imitations of exotic environme conceived in a highly romantic way.

'We visualise and dream', he wrote, 'a magnificent amp theatre under a glorious moonlit sky in an Italian gard in a Persian court, in a Spanish patio, or in a mystic Egyp temple-yard, all canopied by a soft moonlit sky.'

Colour had an important part to play in the interior, b in the auditorium and in the foyer spaces. Of the don ceilings in a typical atmospheric he said, 'we credit the d azure blue of the Mediterranean sky with a therapeu value, soothing the nerves and calming perturbing though

'Prepare Practical Plans for Pretty Playhouses—Please Patrons—Pay Profits' was Eberson's own practical creed. Pretty playhouses were certainly the outcome of his designs, and his desire to 'circumpose' his buildings by 'nature's grand outdoor setting, reproduced in near perfect illusion' came to fruition.

Eberson's first atmospheric was the Majestic at Houston, Texas, opened in 1923. With this design, as Ben Hall suggests, the lid was blown off all the old ideas, for, 'as far as Houstonians of that more innocent day could tell, the Majestic had no roof at all'. But this early theatre, unlike Eberson's later fantastic creations in Chicago, Florida and elsewhere, did not have the fully automatic manufactured weather that it was claimed could 'maintain constant conditions of temperature and humidity in any given closed space'.

Under Eberson's supervision a whole team of experts produced ideas for each project. Eberson in an interview for *Motion Picture News* recalls that inspiration can come from the most unlikely sources.

'Travelling through New Orleans with my friend, Liska, some years ago and attracted by the old-world charm of Royal Street, we rummaged through the antique dealers' shops and spied an ancient pierced brass jewel-studded Persian incense burner. Then and there was born the idea and scheme for a Persian theatre. Persia the land of the turquoise and the rose, the land of the sacred shrine, blue and gold, the predominating colours—a theatre design

developing the auditorium side walls in an interesting non-symmetrical fashion . . .'

Eberson and his associated designers created over hundred of their atmospherics ranging in style from more obscure elements of the Florentine Renaissance complete mock-up of the garden of the Tuileries. Capitol and Paradise Theatres, Chicago, Loew's Parad New York, the Tampa at Tampa, Florida, the Rivi Detroit, and the Olympia, Miami, are just a few outstand examples of Eberson's inventive skill. It was not until 'thirties in England that we could boast (if that is the r word) of anyone who could design pretty cinemas with conviction and aplomb of Eberson. Many tried but fai Only Komisarjevsky came anywhere near success with extravagant interiors for Bernstein's Granada circuit.

On the whole the atmospheric met with derision in Engl and on the Continent and most designers looked to Lan 'hard top' school for inspiration. But it was the sensati Roxy in New York that caught the imagination of the w of cinema designers at the end of the decade. Roxy's dreams materialised when the world's largest, most ma ficent and most expensive movie palace opened in 1 Roxy's name became a household word from the Ameri outback to Lancashire, his memory enshrined for ev an edifice as grand in scale as Garnier's Paris Op Designed by Walter W Ahlschlager of Chicago in c junction with the professional theatre decorator Ha

76

John Eberson's first atmospheric
interior, the Majestic, Houston,
Texas, 1922

busch of New York, the Roxy had everything, a seating ...city of over 6,000, 'decorations of indescribable beauty', ...unda almost the size of a railway station, a square audi-...m as lavish as any royal palace, and mechanical ...pment fit for the largest ocean-going liner. But with all ...t was far from a perfect cinematographic environment. ...hankfully Paul Morand has recorded an impression of ...Cathedral of Motion Pictures' in action in his book, ...York, which clearly conveys much more than a mere ...ription of the architectural quality of the building: ...s for the Roxy, that surpasses the impossible. Find a ...through those dense crowds queued up there all day ...; pass the tall goldlaced ushers, at once door-keepers

and custodians of order; enter this Temple of Solomon. The overheated air is unbreathable, the din of the mechanical orchestra, which one failure in the electricity could bring to a standstill, is merciless—amid palm-trees and gigantic ferns one moves forward into the Mexican palace of some Spanish governor whom the tropics have turned stark mad. The walls are of a reddish rough-cast, treated with a liquid to give a semblance of age, and the brazen doors of the Ark of the Covenant open into a hall with golden cupolas, in old style, and a ceiling with storied panels. Satan has hung this disused sanctuary with scarlet velvet; a nightmare light falls from bowls of imitation alabaster, from yellow glass lanterns, from branching ritual candlesticks; the organ

lamboyant Italianate **cenium of Eberson's** **lise Theatre in the Bronx.**

The *trompe-l'oeil* effect is painted directly onto the asbestos safety curtain

pipes, lit from beneath by greenish lights, make one t
of a cathedral under the waves, and in the walls are ni
awaiting sinful bishops. I find a seat in a deep, soft faut
from which for two hours I witness giant kisses on mo
like the crevasses of the Grand Canyon, embraces of ti
a whole propaganda of the flesh which maddens, wit
satisfying, these violent American temperaments. It is i
than a Black Mass; it is a profanation of everything
music, of art, of love, of colours. I vow I had there a c
plete vision of the end of the world. I saw Broad
suddenly as one vast Roxy, one of those unsubsta
treasures, one of those joy-baited traps, one of those flee
and illusory gifts won by the spells of wicked magici;

By the time the Roxy was finished, American promc
were worrying about the future of motion pictures.

**W. W. Ahlschlager's original
drawings of the Roxy, New York**

...erican architectural magazine expressed this concern— ...The movies—at one time, not so long ago, offering an ...ire program—are being relegated to a position of almost ...nor importance in a program of what might be described ...a new form of theatrical entertainment. The average ...lience in a motion picture theatre today expects a large ...d capable orchestra to play classical selections and "jazz" ...es by turns, and to hear good soloists, or a chorus, with ...borate settings, while it seems to have difficulty in ...ping awake through an uninteresting picture at the ...d of the evening's program . . . The modern motion pic- ...e theatre must prepare for this new form of theatrical ...ertainment.'

...is was what Roxy and colleagues like William Fox

had attempted to do in completing all their schemes with elaborate lighting, large stages and sensational decorations, and most importantly bringing in the talkies and the finest acoustical and projection equipment available at the time. But it still was not enough. Lamb, Eberson, Crane and C W and George Rapp continued to design the same type of basilica-like emporiums to the illusive God of movies. With the opening of the 'fabulous and foolish Fox' in San Francisco in 1929 the golden age of movie palace architecture was closing. Thomas Lamb's design for Fox's own special 'shrine to the world' was in a class of its own, at once absurd, pompous, extravagant and spectacular. It was to display in its construction America's growth and great prosperity and also be the ultimate theatre in Fox's vast movie empire. It was smaller and cheaper to build than

The ground floor plan

ve **The Ladies Lounge in the**
ulous and foolish' **Fox,**
Francisco.

osite **North Wall of the main**
itorium. **Legend has it that a**
re ornate treatment' **was**
inally proposed by the architect.

**A detail of one of the side exits
and the north wall of the main
auditorium of the Fox**

Roxy's Theatre in New York but nothing was spared in an attempt to make it the most appropriate home of the movies on the West Coast.

It cost $5,000,000 to construct and seated 5,000 people, Within three years it had closed and Fox himself was bankrupt. Its rebirth the following year under the control of the West Coast Fox Organisation saw it struggling for custom from the 30-cent public. But even with low prices its glory was eclipsed and according to Jeff Hershel, in his monograph on the theatre, *Fabulous and Foolish Fox*, it virtually impossible to fill it to capacity. 'Al Jolson, v lost more money for the box office than any other perforr at that time, declared that "there was a herd of loose Indi located in the balcony".'

The rise and fall of the Fox was symptomatic of the c dition of the American film industry at the time. It was last grand gesture by the omnipotent promoter before Depression, the close of a great but short-lived era.

The British cinema
in the twenties

In Britain the First World War and the subsequent restrictions on building made the development of the cinema impossible during the years 1914–20.

In the period immediately following the war American companies completely dominated the British market. With film production at a very low ebb in Britain the American renters exploited the market to the full. They introduced methods of 'blind' and block booking and eventually forced British promoters in the early 'twenties to speed up their own building activity. In the *Kine Year Book 1921* it was estimated that the number of 4,000 low-seating capacity houses should be increased by another 2,000 in order that a new market could be created for British productions.

When the wartime restrictions on building were lifted after 1920 it became possible to erect a new type of cinema building which provided the public with the comfort and quality of design it had begun to demand in the pre-war period. However, even with this concern to build more cinemas of a superior type for British films, the cinema-going public still showed a distinct preference for American productions. The desire for the American story film and the obvious assimilation of American ideas for the design of cinema buildings created difficulties for the indigenous film-makers. In terms of design the cinema in the United States had progressed a great deal during the war years and compared with their American counterparts English architects found themselves far behind in matters of planning and decoration. English architects also found themselves behind in matters of presentation techniques.

One of the first major cinemas to appear in this cou after the war was the Regent, Brighton (1921), desig by Robert Atkinson, a highly respected architect teacher. Atkinson brought his considerable knowledg architecture and building construction to bear on a building type which he considered to be one of the g challenges to the imagination of architects in the twent century. Before 1914 he had been in partnership George Alexander, who had erected picture house Edinburgh, Liverpool and elsewhere. Alexander was k in the war and the practice continued in Atkinson's na The Brighton Regent was the most important of his e commissions and the first in line of many later 'Su cinemas'. Situated on an awkward site it was designed an interesting auditorium approached from entrance various levels. This pioneer English cinema was a di result of the experience Atkinson had gained by study at first hand new theatres in America. It set a high stand of functional efficiency for a type of building that struggling to find an identity of its own.

The picture theatre of the post-war era was based on legitimate theatre. It was a scaled enlargement of theatres and music halls of the late nineteenth cent Architects took their ideas from existing theatre build and saw the whole development of buildings for the mo as a natural extension of theatre requirements. 'After Robert Atkinson asked, 'is not the picture theatre a deve

87

The New Adelphi, Swinton.
Two interior views

architect's drawing for an
al Egyptian style interior
916

Egyptian style front of The
iera, Manchester

ment and an advance on normal theatre designing? . . . the moving picture has overtaken the theatre, passed it, and incidentally applied to theatre design the impetus which conservatism and lethargy in design had stifled almost to death, at any rate in England.'

In a paper given to the Royal Institute of British Architects in 1921, from which the foregoing extracts have been taken, Robert Atkinson complained that few architects of first-rate ability were being employed on the design of cinemas in England. This may have been due, he said, to two factors, firstly that the picture house was beneath the notice of the heads of the profession, and secondly that the promoters lacked selective ability. This gradually changed during the decade as the industry and the new promoters saw the benefit of seeking competent professional advice on individual buildings that were exceptionally expensive and needed imaginative and expert planning. The ideas of a decade or so before had been amateurish to say the least and architects—if they were used at all—had struggled with the whims of clients whose only wish seemed to be for an external visual extravaganza and a bare interior.

In Atkinson's heyday the emphasis changed and architects produced their logical and well-ordered plans, only to get lost again in the decoration and a plethora of stylistic details. The new functional architecture had barely touched England's shores and the only way to solve the façade and decoration problem for most architects was to deal with the design of picture theatres as a series of preconceived stylistic notions, using the models of the Greek and Roman theatres and of the dreamt-up styles of the lesser known Assyrian, Chinese and Egyptian examples. The *Art Nouveau* —dead as a style by this time, but still popular with some Continental theatre architects—received little recognition in England even from the designers who had read *The Studio* or visited the *fin de siècle* pubs. The style that seemed really to capture the imagination of architecture in England in the early 'twenties was the Egyptian. Sir Thomas Bennett referred to the style as impressive with a massive and 'almost superhuman quality'. One of the earliest attempts to produce a new architecture of monumentality based on the Egyptian style was Adelaide House, near London Bridge, by Sir John Burnet and Partners, erected between 1921 and 1924. The Arcadia Works for Carreras in Camden Town, erected in 1926, also found its expression through reinforced concrete Neo-Egyptian facades.

The origins of the Egyptian style cinema therefore a precedent in contemporary practice as well as a histo one—in London at least—in the famous Egyptian Hall had stood in Piccadilly for nearly a century. The n façade of the Carlton, Islington (1930), designed by Ge Coles, was clearly derived from this source.

In America Sid Grauman built his Egyptian Theatr Hollywood in 1922. This was designed by the archit Meyer and Holler and was meant to outdo even the n opulent pharaoh. The stage, Ben Hall writes, 'made K Tut's tomb look like the old family burial vault'.

The Streatham Astoria, built in 1930 and designec A E Stone, was less opulent than Grauman's Egyp but it made up for this in sheer size, the stage alone b

The Carlton, Islington, c 1930

er than that of Drury Lane. The auditorium, which
ed 3,000 people, was a blaze of red and gold. The huge
ging ceiling covered the stalls and circle and spanned
een two arches, one at the proscenium end and the
r at the balcony end of the building. The proscenium
ning curved out from the front arch and above this the
ilation was neatly fitted in. In keeping with the hieratic
ptian style bas-relief on the side walls of the circle the
ains resembled a gigantic Egyptian tapestry.

later example in the provinces, the Pyramid (now
on) at Sale (1933), designed by Drury and Gomersall,
a complete essay in Egyptian detailing, while the
ous columns of the Riviera, Manchester, also clearly
Karnak.

Pavilion, Shepherd's Bush, 1923

Many of the technical problems that designers had to
solve are dealt with in a later chapter but it is worth men-
tioning here that architects had to modify their ideas on
the traditional theatre on two points straight away. The
most expensive theatre seats are those in the front row, for
the obvious reason that this is the best position to hear what
the actors are saying and see their features. The movies
demand a reversal of this in order that the distortion of the
picture is reduced. The other factor is the one of theatre
shape; with the cinema the architect had to plan with
projection and vision lines in mind and not just erect
rectangular walls and numerous high balconies to house
his audience.

Robert Atkinson, in his RIBA paper referred to previously, provided an excellent summary of picture theatre practice up to the year 1921. He visualised the perfect audience
size for a theatre to be in the region of 1,500 people in a one-
storey building and up to 3,000 people on an expensive site
with a double-storey auditorium. The three-tier theatre he
considered to be quite useless for reasons of vision. He
found the ideal plan to be fan-shaped with a conical outline
in section, which indeed became popular on the Continent.

No consistent aesthetic emerged in the early picture houses
either externally or in the public spaces inside. Anything
was allowed, colonnaded fronts, colossal ceilings with heavy
coffers, giant arched proscenium openings, elaborate can-
delabra, and over-emphasised entrance doorways. Stylism
ran wild.

Typical of the British cinemas of the early 'twenties were
the Savoy Cinema, Uxbridge, and the Ayr Picture House
(designed by Lennox and MacMath), both of which opened
in 1922. The Uxbridge cinema was disguised as a Georgian
Town House, with stock brick elevations and a red-tiled
roof. Inside, the ground floor accommodated 666 and the
balcony 348 people. The overall size of the building was
140 feet by 31 feet 6 inches. The Ayr Picture House was
slightly more elaborate possessing the usual Scottish tea-
room and in this case using that space for a foyer as well.
The walls were solid brick and the floors constructed in
reinforced concrete which was unusual in picture house
design at that time. The building was 180 feet long by
66 feet wide with a tiered ground floor and a minute balcony.

One of the first major cinemas of real architectural interest in England was the Shepherd's Bush Pavilion, de-

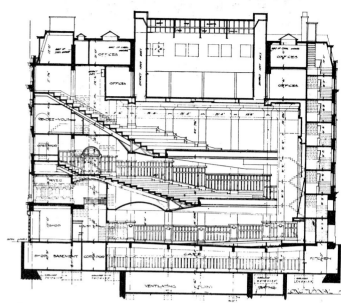

signed by Frank T Verity and opened in 1923. At a time when the architectural profession as a whole considered the civic value of a cinema building to be exceedingly low it is surprising to find that this building won the RIBA London Street Architecture Award for 'the best frontage completed during the year 1923' within a radius of four miles of Charing Cross. The distinguished jury for the award, which included Sir Edwin Lutyens and Mr (later Sir) Guy Dawber, found the Pavilion an 'imposing structure of brick and stone in which the former material especially is used with great imagination'. Built allegedly in the 'American/Roman manner' it was indeed a great step forward in English cinema design although its interior was little more than an emasculated version of a typical music hall. It had been designed during the war years, but due to restrictions on building it was not possible to build it before 1922. Commercially the Pavilion was a great success even though the idea of erecting a 3,000-seat theatre was considered by many people a doubtful proposition. The Davis Family, who had earlier built the Highgate Pavilion in 1910 and the sumptuous Marble Arch Pavilion in 1914, did not share the views of the pessimists and boldly claimed that within six months they were playing films to an average audience of 25,000 people a week.

It is worth comparing the Pavilion with the large Manchester Piccadilly Picture Theatre (now Littlewood's store) erected in 1922. This building—the first of the grand scale cinemas in the North of England—had an elegant, almost Parisian frontage and an auditorium seating 1,000 people. The basic shape of the building was ▯ angular but with two semi-circular balconies curving r▯ the three sides of the high auditorium. The semi-circ▯ shape of the balconies was reflected also in the plain ▯ of the proscenium.

In the mid-twenties English architects were almost c▯ pletely unaware of Continental developments where ▯ the war the search had been for a distinctive and 'mod▯ architecture, a point that is made very clear if a fur▯ comparison is made between English picture theatres of ▯ time and the work, say, of Wilms or Poelzig in German▯ Gunnar Asplund's Skandia Cinema in Stockholm of ▯

What inspiration English designers had was drawn f▯ the Americans in general and from Thomas Lamb ▯ John Eberson in particular. Lamb's early and rather h▯ Adam-esque structures were considered to be both ta▯ fully designed and proportionally acceptable by his Eng▯ counterparts. The English tendency towards tradition ▯ conventional architectural values only changed tow▯ the end of the 'thirties. This was due very largely to ▯ evangelising activity of one man, P Morton Shand. Sh▯ was not an architect but he was completely enamoure▯ the Modern Movement and the progress its pioneers ▯ made on the Continent. In articles in the *Architect▯ Review* from 1929 onwards he exhorted English archit▯ to follow the lead of their Continental *confrères*. He ▯ biting in his attacks on the appalling taste of English cine▯

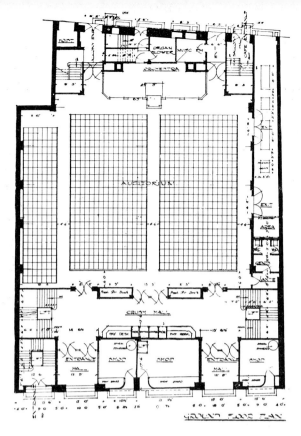

GROUND FLOOR PLAN

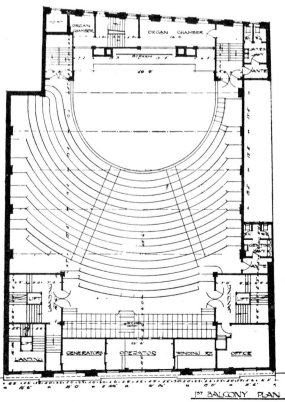

1ST BALCONY PLAN

Abbeydale Picture Theatre,
Sheffield, 1922

designers in his book, *Modern Theatres and Cinemas,* which was published by Batsford in 1930. 'At the end of the war', he wrote, 'the film had sufficiently perfected its technique for almost unlimited possibilities to lie before it . . . cinemas began to be built in England . . . here, there and everywhere, to any sort of design, and often to no design at all. English theatres and music halls had rarely been built by qualified architects. The bad tradition was continued with the cinema'. In another piece of writing, an article in the *Ideal Kinema* in 1931, he goes further:

'Clearly all that had to be done (in the design of a cinema) was to imitate the United States, the home of jazz, and all big and fruity things.'

Morton Shand was harshly critical of cinema architects in England but the force of his overstated arguments was taken to heart. For too long the ridicule of professional critics was directed towards the amateur designer, to the man who had managed to obtain a commission but had not the technical skill nor the imagination to carry out the work. Shand's comments were clearly directed towards the exhibitors in the 1920's who did not know who the competent designers were. The situation was clearly summed up in an Editorial in *The Architects' Journal* :

'The design of our cinemas is part of the heavy price we pay for our public neglect of architecture and our national indifference to the now patent fact that architecture is the only one of the arts which has not as yet succeeded in expressing the modern spirit.

The desire of the film-exhibitor being usually to guise his picture theatre as a showman's booth, it is surprising that British architects have so far had no adeq chance of trying to discover the cinema's most logical satisfactory structural form. For one thing they are relati seldom employed.'

Of the architects who were involved in cinema desig the 1920s the firm of Leathart and Granger stand ou particular mention. Shand singled out Julian Leatha 'our foremost cinema architect' and his view is corrobor by the amount of space and comment the work of architect had in the technical and cinema press at the t

. Leathart's own views on architecture were expresse lectures, articles and later in his book *Style in Architec* published in 1940. His position was essentially that of middle-of-the-road modernist. His cinemas therefore about them a traditional appearance with a marked duction in decorative motifs and fiddling details.

With his partner W F Granger, Leathart designed bold Kensington Cinema in the High Street. When it built in 1926 it was claimed to be the largest cinem England with a seating capacity of just over 2,300. exterior remains a fine composition, Classical in origin austere and controlled by the use of a deeply rece entrance. Internally it was less confident. The vast balc sweeps down over the stalls but the feeling it gives is of a cinema and more of a cross between a Roman bas and a non-conformist preaching house, with its high heav

94

Kensington, London, 1926.
auditorium and the main
e

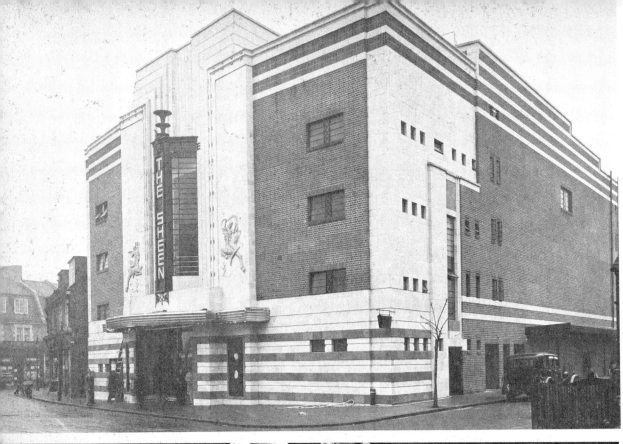

The Sheen Cinema, interior
and main front

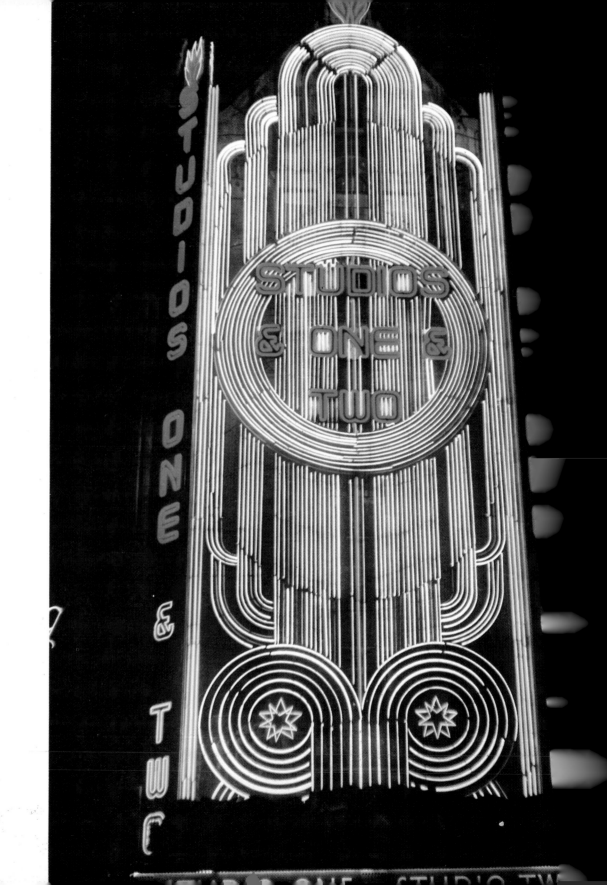

Studios One and Two, Oxford
Street, London, 1936

2 Astoria, Finsbury Park–
proscenium

3 Astoria, Finsbury Park–
plasterwork detailing to the
circle foyer

fered ceiling and rectangular plan. The Kensington, as designers admitted five years later, was at the extreme of the gamut of styles. The end, in fact, that came to a stop. 'It has all the paraphernalia of the Neo-Grec', athart wrote, 'coffers, entablatures, frets, rondels and rest of the characteristic features of this style'.

The Twickenham Cinema (1929) and the Sheen (1930) e more confident examples of cinema design produced the same firm. The Sheen (now demolished) took into ount the advances in exterior lighting and was the first lor contribution to English 'night architecture'. Leath-s Richmond Cinema closely followed the pattern of rent American practice and had one of the first semi-ospheric interiors in the London area. It simulated, at at cost, a Spanish/American courtyard. The £10,000 omatic colour-change lighting installation created, gedly, 'varying simulations from dawn to nightfall by cealed lighting on the top of the loggias to a plain un-orated ceiling'. As one would expect, this 'outside-in' tment of the auditorium drove Shand to accuse Leathart going 'over to the enemy' with his efforts at 'architec-lised acoustics'.

The work of Leathart and Granger presaged the super-ema in England. The 'big' cinema had begun to replace palatial examples in cities throughout the country and appearance of vast new edifices had become a common ure in the London area by 1930. The Carlton, Hay-rket, designed by Frank Verity, the Plaza, Haymarket, E A Stone, the Regent, Bournemouth, and Green's yhouse in Glasgow (with 4,400 seats the largest cinema Europe in the late 'twenties), were among the first mples of the cathedral-type buildings that were to be a nmon feature in most major towns in the next decade.

The 'Golden Age' of the American cinema building urred in the 'twenties. In Britain, the boom years were n 1928–1938 when the cinema architect had things more own way and the talkies had arrived. This had been made sible only by the intervention of the Government and passing of the *Cinematograph Films Act* of 1927. With-this Act the British cinema would have surely died. e years 1927–1930 have been called 'the watershed ween "medieval and modern" film history' in the PEP ort on the British Film Industry. The same can be l of cinema building history. The best and the most :inctively modern buildings were yet to come.

The semi-atmospheric interior of the Richmond Cinema

Overleaf **The Carlton, Haymarket, London**

CARLTON

THOSE MAGNIFICENT MEN IN THEIR FLYING MACHINES
— OR HOW I FLEW FROM LONDON TO PARIS IN 25 HOURS AND 11 MINUTES

ONE WAY STREET

7

The advent of the talkies

The Search for Synchronisation

Although the Talkies did not become a commercial success until 1927, work had been carried out on combining motion pictures with words and music even before the film industry began. Dickson, in Edison's laboratory, linked an early peepshow machine with one of the newly invented phonographs as early as 1888. This was not very successful for, as Terry Ramsaye has written in *A Million and One Nights*, all he managed to get out of the combination was 'one cylinder of fairly good sound and one full of frightful pictures'. For a short time these machines were produced commercially, but they did not last. The coupling of the Kinetoscope with a phonograph was equally unsuccessful.

Eugène Lauste was the first inventor to patent a Talkie Film Machine that worked reasonably well and this was a result of combining the projection equipment developed by Frieze-Green with the ideas on sound and light he had learnt from the German scientist Ruhmer. By 1906 he was exhibiting films with a sound track that operated a photo-electric cell in an ingenious projector.

Lauste set the pattern for all future development. John Scotland wrote in his book, *The Talkies*, 'Lauste's ingenuity was really extraordinary . . . there was no fundamental feature of Talkie work that his British patents did not cover'. Unfortunately, due to personal difficulties Lauste allowed his patents to lapse and he lost the opportunity of seeing his ideas prove commercially profitable to himself. However, his machines were copied and used by many of the big film companies after his death in 1

Before it became entirely feasible to link film with recorded sound a number of experiments had been m and these were tried out on the paying public.

The 'Illusion of Life' Technique

In 1907 Harry Lauder's voice accompanied the show of films in which he acted. For sixteen weeks this pheno enal performance was given every day at the Lon Hippodrome. While the artist could be seen singing on screen, talking machines reproduced his voice throug chronophone—or a chronomegaphone in large hall capturing what the promoters called at the time the 'illu of life'.

The Cinephone and Vivaphone

The Cinephone and the Vivaphone were very similar ty of systems used for an elementary kind of sound and synchronisation. In Barker's Cinephone each scene acted firstly in front of a recording phonograph and t re-enacted in front of the camera to match that record For showing the films a projector was adjusted so tha ran at the same fixed speed as the phonograph. Or at l that is what it was meant to do. The phongraph had a sm dial, like a clock-face, which was placed in an illumina position near the screen. The projected film had a sim clock-faced dial in the bottom left-hand corner. As film proceeded the phonograph played and the ha

ated around the dial. The ambidextrous projectionist
=n had the job of matching the dials. The human element
=n defeated this method!

Cecil Hepworth's Vivaphone was somewhat simpler than
= Cinephone. It relied on matching sound and vision
=ough a single indicator and the use of coloured glass.
=hen the indicator—powered by an electro-magnet—
=s vertical all was well, but when it showed red the
=chine had to be speeded up and when green it had to be
=wed down.

Gaumont invented a further method in 1910 which was
= improvement on a system first tried out in 1902, and
=hough this method relied on the distribution of loud-
=eakers throughout the auditorium it failed largely through
=tortion.

e Vitaphone

=e success of the 'Talkies' was due to the Warner
=others, who, finding themselves nearly bankrupt in 1925,
=ided to produce sound-on-disc movies. Using first of all
=lent film, *Don Juan,* they recorded a musical accompani-
=nt. It was not successful. In 1927 they decided to gamble
= the real thing, a film in which words and music fitted
=t of the actual story. *The Jazz Singer* was the result, with
=Jolson, the king of the chocolate-coloured coons, gushing
= the words of his songs. The system used for this film—
=veloped by the Western Electric Company of America—
=s called the 'Vitaphone'. It consisted of 16-inch gramo-

phone records each synchronised with separate reels of
film. *The Jazz Singer* and *The Singing Fool* were the first
universally successful talkies. The Warner Brothers' innovation caused the industry as a whole to quicken its pace
and within a short time the first examples of sound recorded
directly on film were introduced by Fox-Case. They went
under the trade name of 'Movietone'. Many other novel
methods of producing sound on film were used—including
the variable density method favoured by British Talking
Pictures—but they all employed the basic principles
devised by Western Electric.

By 1928, with sound synchronised to moving pictures,
the new word *Talkies* had found a firm place in English
usage. 'See and *Hear* Movies' became a catchpenny phrase.
The talkies added a new dimension to the cinema palace
and brought to light the black science of a new expert,
the acoustics engineer. He was joined by the consultant
fibrous plaster decorator. With the coming of sound the
old barn-like structures were soon outdated and as it proved
impossible to adapt them acoustically to the new medium
they soon lost favour with the patrons, who wanted to hear
properly as well as view the film in comfortable surroundings. Difficulties arose immediately, not only over the
existing shape of larger buildings—in which patrons
quickly noticed deficiencies in sound quality—but also
with the reproducing methods themselves. Many exhibitors
found them too expensive to install and on top of this the
first systems themselves were by no means ideal acoustic-

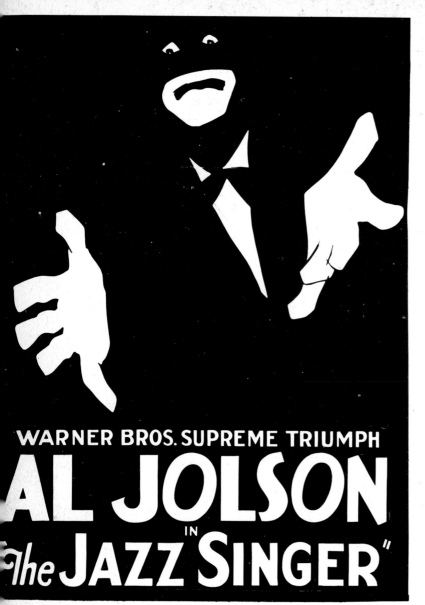

A contemporary poster for an
Al Jolson talkie

loudspeakers in about 1930. It was possible with this n
sound reproducing method to focus and unify the sou
and beam it to various parts of the auditorium.

The talkies created an immediate demand for a new ty
of auditorium: an acoustic box, muffled to keep t
sound in and protected to stop noise penetrating from o
side. It proved to be the most fundamental change
cinema design since the industry began.

In the rush of enthusiasm for the talkies both exhibit
and designers mistakenly thought that auditoria could be
large as they cared to make them. One magazine in 1
reported that 'there is every inducement—psychologi
commercial and mechanical—to build cinemas larger a
larger'. The argument put forward was that the earl
limit of the power of the human voice in the legitim
theatre had been adopted in cinema design practice
with the advent of the talkies it was no longer a reasona
criterion for the size of a building. The big building ca
into vogue and the industry strode boastfully into
'thirties erecting 'supers', 'super-palaces' and 'super-
luxe' cinemas by the hundred. In 1929 over three hu
dred new cinemas were either under construction or p
posed, while in London alone fifteen new super cinen
were fitted out to show sound and stereoscopic films. T
theme at the opening of this, the Second Cinema A
according to an Editorial in *The Builder* in 1929, was ba
on the assumption that the design of buildings for
talkies was 'not a question of art but psychology'.

ally. In some cinemas audiences were fortunate if they
caught one word in three, for generally the early talkies
were played far too loud. The effects of this, plus side wall
echoes and 'standing' waves, made a visit to the cinema an
uncomfortable experience. The breakthrough came with
the invention of the multi-cellular high frequency horn

The era of the 'super' cinema

The 'super' cinema was a direct result of the attempt by exhibitors and designers to provide the cinema-goer with greater 'illusion', elegance and comfort in their buildings. Generally, the English examples were less extravagant than their American prototypes, although many of them were designed for equally large audiences.

The success of Frank Verity's Pavilion at Shepherd's Bush in the early 'twenties, both commercially and architecturally, clearly influenced the whole thinking behind the supers. Indeed Verity himself was responsible for pioneering what was later called the 'super-de-luxe' in this country. He—with his partner S Beverley—acted as European advisor to the Paramount Company, designing for them the Plaza, Regent Street, the Paramounts in Paris and in London's Tottenham Court Road, as well as 'key' cinemas in the provinces at Manchester, Newcastle, Glasgow and Birmingham. The firm was also responsible for many smaller buildings for the Union Cinema Company.

Frank Verity's training stood him in good stead for the design of cinema buildings. He had studied architecture in London at the Royal College of Art, University College, the Architectural Association, the Royal Academy Schools, and in Paris. The son of an architect, he was destined for a very successful career. His wide practice included commissions for the main frontage to the Regent Street Polytechnic, Lord's grandstand and important apartment buildings in Mayfair. But he is best remembered—he died in 1937—for his many and varied theatres such as Mrs

Langtry's Imperial, Westminster, the Empire, Leice Square, the Scala, Charlotte Street, the Theatre Ro Windsor, and the Theatre Royal, Bath. It was th buildings that led inevitably to his employment as the 'specialist' picture theatre architect.

Unfortunately two of his largest cinema buildings, Plaza and the Carlton, were decorated rather too thi in rich Italian details and consequently they dated v quickly. Verity had, however, created a new standarc finish and quality that was to be emulated by all colleagues.

The Shepherd's Bush Pavilion, which had been built Israel Davis, had shown that the large-scale theatre-cin was commercially feasible. It is not surprising to fi therefore, that the first palatial suburban super had Davis circuit behind it. Plans were put forward by Davis, for the erection of a major suburban giant at Croy early in 1927. By the time the work on the theatre had be the circuit had amalgamated with the Bromhea Gaumont-British Corporation. The project went forw as planned and was called the Davis' Theatre. Designec Robert Cromie, the man who was to become the *doye* independent British cinema architects, building work be in October 1927. When it opened its doors to the pu fourteen months later the theatre was described as the n ambitious project of its kind in Europe. Today the Dav the cream of the supers, has gone, replaced by the cc mercial buildings of the present time.

The theatre had opened just at the time of the introduction of the talkies in England. It had been designed for
full stage use, and the plan included a small lake under the
boards and a large pit for full orchestral support to the silent
films. It was intended that programmes should be planned
to a pattern of 'picture—music—stage', each part complete
in itself. The talkies changed this original emphasis and
for many years it was used for separate cinema and theatre
shows.

The vast auditorium of the Davis' was decorated completely in 'modern French decorative work' and surmounted
by a 50 foot diameter reflective dome. The ancillary accommodation—foyers, vestibules and cloakrooms—was
grouped around a spacious rotunda finished internally with
a coloured marble mosaic.

Externally the main front was dressed in portland stone
with centrally grouped windows in gilded cast iron, very
much in the Thomas Lamb manner.

A month before the Davis' Theatre opened in Croydon
the first Regal Cinema in London came into operation at
Marble Arch. Built, as the programme said, 'for English-
men, with English materials' it stood, somewhat paradoxically, as the programme goes on to explain, on the site used
by the Roman Legions to guard the Tyburn on the corner
of the Edgware Road. Its decoration therefore was not in the
English tradition but in a contrived Roman style. The main
scheme was designed by Clifford Aish and the design for
the interior was chosen from sketches submitted by forty

artists in competition. You were meant to feel regal at
Regal. No expense was spared. Passenger lifts took patr
from the principal entrances to all floors—to the dance
the tea rooms and the circle.

The interior decoration of the auditorium was based
the colours of a spray of autumn leaves from Burnh
Beeches provided by the Managing Director, A E Abraha
Colours matching these leaves, gold, brown and red, w
used throughout the auditorium which was based o
Roman amphitheatre, 'with glades of trees and garland
creepers visible in autumnal guise through a grac
colonnade'. The foliage was carried out in bas-relief.
proscenium was ornamented with 'vigorous acanthus
designs' while the cove above the proscenium arch
picted Dawn; and on either side fountains flanked
ornate organ grilles. A massive pergola was situated in
roof space, where, to continue from the ridiculous p
gramme notes, the 'trails of golden creeper twine, catch
the truant sunbeams as they pass . . . The Centre of
Temple has a coffered beam, which carries the Perg
supported by a wall with a pilaster and Roman tripod, a
the glade continues right round to the doorways, which
embraced in the Roman scheme'. When the gold curta
were drawn back a simple rectangle in white, of Div
Proportions, could be seen against a black background
must have been a relief !

The Regal and the Davis' were essentially one-
'tailor-made' buildings, unlike the famous London Asto

Davis' Theatre, Croydon.
rchitect's original drawing
e front

v The luxurious interior of
Regal, Marble Arch

which were variations on a single Atmospheric theme. These have a significant place in British movie building history that is only comparable with the mammoth Granadas decorated by Komisarjevsky. The four main Astorias in London, at Brixton, Finsbury Park, Streatham and the Old Kent Road, were all designed by the circuit architect Edward A Stone in association with T R Somerford.

These cinemas, the English version of the American 'Palaces of Light', were built on a grand scale. As blatant American imports they mimicked Eberson's work in Houston and Chicago. They were also the poor-man's Roxy. Strategically placed in working-class suburbs their interiors were an extravagant, luxurious contrast to their surrounding. They can only be compared with the interiors of the more ostentatious Roman Catholic churches that were another common feature of the poorer suburbs. Roxy's epithet, 'the Cathedral of Motion Pictures', can be used again to describe the Astorias, for the faithful thousands came into the houses transformed by the gods of commercialism and were filled with awe and wonder and immediately involved in the liturgy of the silver screen.

The first of the Astorias was built at Brixton on a corner site in Stockwell Road. Completed in 1929 it held an audience of 4,500. The main façade, which today looks exactly the same as when it was built, is in green and cream terra-cotta with an ambitious copper-covered semi-dome over the main entrance lobby. Stylistically it is a blend of Egyptian and Classical motifs. The splayed auditorium is frankly Italian with a garden simulating, as the architect desired, a 'pleasing' natural scene. The whole of the atmospheric treatment of the auditorium is best viewed from balcony level, where, quoting Ian Cameron, the patrons 'could look down at the monumental doorways and pergolas dripping with plaster vines, ahead to a flattened miniature of the rialto along the top of the proscenium arch, sideways to the walls topped with statues under the Lombardy poplars, seen against the sky'. The Brenograph Junior projected the effects of dawn and dusk, stars and clouds, on the smooth coved ceiling and it is said that an automaton moved across the rialto bridge, in front of the full-size stage.

The auditorium of the Astoria at Finsbury Park featured a Moorish walled city and was even more ambitious than the Brixton example. Great plaster lions peered menacingly

Above and right **The Astoria, Brixton with its half-dome entrance hall**

down at the audience from the sides of the red-brick proscenium arch. The sides of the arch were the main gatep to a gold and crimson velvet-curtained opening thro which the patrons were drawn into the city of mo pictures. The walls surrounding the other parts of auditorium were originally in a checker-board patt coloured in light red and yellow ochre. After the show starry-eyed audience, having experienced the splendo of the proscenium arch and the deep evening blue atm pheric sky, returned to the cooling effects of the foun court, with its illuminated fountain finished in gold black mosaic and set in a star-shaped surround. It indeed splendour in Finsbury Park.

In the Egyptian-inspired Astoria at Streatham the t effect was a little less disturbing. Built originally a semi-atmospheric, with a reduction of decorative mo all round, it has now been reduced to a conventional Od after the interior was ruined by fire.

The Old Kent Road Astoria (1930), also designed E A Stone, represents the trend towards simplicity s further. It is much smoother inside than the other Astor much better acoustically, has no pre-auditorium frills is a solidly-massed building externally. It resembles

of Lamb, and consequently Frank Verity, much more
that of Eberson. But it is fair to assume that like many
urban cinemas it is really neither one thing nor the
, neither flat-topped nor frilly. Perhaps the designers
running out of ideas? If so, then the continuity of
n ideas for super auditoria, if any progression existed,
n the hands of Bernstein Theatres Ltd., whose key
ner dominated the next stage.

isarjevsky and Granada
dore Komisarjevsky was the chief exponent in England
e 'fibrous-plaster cake' type of interior decoration.
y well-known for his work on theatre sets Komisar-

jevsky took less enthusiastically at first to the job of creating
stage designs inside a cinema. In fact, his experience of
theatre work throughout Europe made him altogether
critical of the value and purpose of the commercial cinema.
Not for Komisarjevsky the simulation of nature by the
use of artificial lighting and stucco trees, his aim was to
achieve 'decorative harmony' in style and with taste.

In his designs he aimed to provide entertainment for the
patrons, in the entrance hall, the foyer and in the auditorium.
The picture theatre, he wrote, 'supplies folk with the
flavour of romance for which they crave. The richly decorated theatre, the comfort with which they are surroun-
ded, the efficiency of the service contribute to an atmosphere

The Astoria, Finsbury Park. The
ground floor plan, exterior and
fountain court

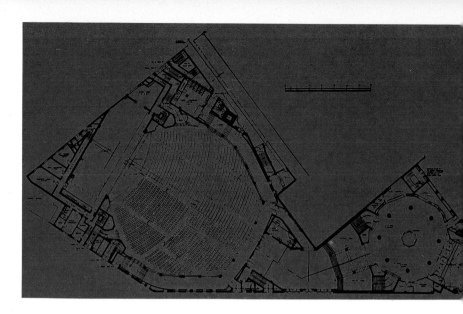

atmospheric interior of
Astoria, Charing Cross Road

and a sense of well-being of which the majority have hitherto only imagined. While there they can with reason consider themselves as good as anyone, and are able to enjoy their cigarettes or their little love affairs in comfortable seats and amidst attractive and appealing surroundings.'

Komisarjevsky was not directly opposed to the German *Sachlichkeit* method of decoration, with its simple forms, use of natural materials and concealed lighting, but he was convinced that it had a limited use in theatre decoration. By eschewing the functional he was left with the eclectic. He attempted to give his interiors a stylistic face-lift—creating an *impression* of a style or a place and not a slavish *reproduction*. He adopted an imaginative composition made up of the elements of a style, 'similar to what in music is called a "paraphrase", that would harmonise with the proportions of the construction, and would suggest the . . . style and give its atmosphere to the theatre'. The decoration of the main auditorium itself was his forte.

Komisarjevsky put his stylistic ideas into operation in the decoration of the Granada at Dover in 1930. Writing about this building later he boasted, 'I succeeded in producing an effect of architectural harmony, of richness, and at the same time of restfulness'. The building was decorated in the motifs of the Moorish style with echoes of the real Alhambra Palace at Granada here and there. In its way it was an artistic success and won the decorator much praise from members of the cinema industry. He again used this

Moorish style in the decoration of the Granada, Walth stow, but this time traces of the palace of Cordoba to be found mixed with seventeenth century Spa Baroque details.

In 1933 Komisarjevsky produced the interior schem the reconstruction of the Empire, Edmonton, for Si Bernstein. Originally built in 1908 to the design of (Massey, then an assistant to Bertie Crewe, the thematic developed by Komisarjevsky was 'ultra-modern'. mirrors, futuristic designs of bright colours on the colur staircases and balustrades all added up to an interior suggested the blocky, rectangular work of the Dutc *Stijl*—but lacked its spirit.

More successful were Komisarjevsky's well-know teriors for the Granadas at Tooting and Woolwich (19 both designed in conjunction with the architects (Massey and R H Uren. Both auditoria were of similar portions and both had the same main features, a po Neo-Gothic arch over the emergency exit doors on e side of the proscenium, and highly-coloured coff ceilings. The Woolwich Granada, which remains in e lent condition, was described at the time it was open 'the most romantic theatre ever built' with its mixtu Continental Gothic motifs.

Externally this large building—seating 3,000 peop gives little indication of its exotic interior. It has a curved brickwork street frontage with a tower featu canopy and simple Granada lettering. The first visual s

anada, Tooting—part of
neo-gothic interior

verleaf) Foyer of the Old
Theatre, San Francisco

The strange contrast of styles at the Granada, Woolwich. A period interior (by Komisarjevsky) forms a strange contrast to the 'modernistic' exterior of the building. Architects: Cecil Massey and R. H. Uren

comes to the patrons after paying their money and entering the foyer. Out of this space a staircase, decorated with golden gothic arches on the wall behind the landing and lit from concealed floods, leads up to the circle and restaurant. Once up at balcony level the patron could at one time either go into the restaurant or through the puce and pink Moorish 'hall of mirrors' (now a casino) to the auditorium, the decorative climax itself. Inside, the heavy arches are prominent and the complexity of colour, contour, lighting and detailing still draw the astonished 'ahs' and 'ughs' when the house lights go up. One unusual feature at stalls level is the carved wooden balustrade that runs around three sides of the auditorium for the use of standees. At one time, amid all this artificial splendour, Reginald Dixon rumbled out his popular melodies on the mighty Wurlitzer.

The Tooting Granada, which also retains its former glory, if not its former popularity, is no less exotic than the one at Woolwich. The foyer was designed as a mock Baronial hall with a minstrels' gallery. In this cinema Komisarjevsky again used the 'hall of mirrors' to create a dreamland for the benefit of waiting customers.

The 'Super' Architect

The demand for larger cinema buildings accelerated in the early 'thirties; at times it seemed almost insatiable. Owners frantically sought for architects and designers to carry out their work. Often they attempted to persuade architects to cut considerably their standard fees. Designers who did

take on work on this basis were recompensed with b of shares or some other system of profit-sharing; ot turned down enormous amounts of work in order to r their professional integrity.

Many of the architects who did become involved the film industry had previous experience in theatre concert-hall design. A large number of offices had t reorganised to cope with the unprecedented deman the new industry—novel ideas for façade treatment interior decoration had to be thought up and drawn o great speed. Buildings shot up virtually overnight architects were afraid of being seen surveying pos sites because of the tendency of landowners to inc their prices once it was known that a plot had 'cir potential'.

With the demand for new cinemas the individu architect came into his own. Established reputations enhanced by the erection of successful super cinemas many a young practitioner made his name during phase. The names that did not get into the panels of on the front of their buildings include George C Harry W Weedon, Andrew Mather, Cecil Howitt, Shennan, W E Trent, Drury and Gomersall, as w the names already mentioned, Verity and Beverly, Cr Stone and Massey.

George Cole's first colossal cinema building wa Trocadero, opened at the Elephant and Castle in 193 designed for H and G Kinemas Ltd. This *Cafedral o*

osite **The ambitiously coffered**
ng of the Granada, Tooting

ve **The much less ambitious**
refined interior of a standard
nada at Bedford

The Trocadero, Elephant and Castle, London. The exterior.

movies was a truly elephantine essay in Italian Renaissance period decoration. Built for the talkies the *Troc* brought three hours of Piccadilly luxury and comfort to the patron for the price of a big sandwich. The interior, carefully planned to lie diagonally across a difficult site, was most impressive spatially with a vast balcony cutting the volume almost in two. The proscenium curved up to meet the ceiling and running round the walls of the auditorium tall alcoves emphasised the enormous height of the space. The other accommodation—stage and dressing rooms, heavily-

mirrored waiting rooms and lifts—was fused to the au torium shape but did not impinge on the pilastered pedimented terra-cotta external elevations, which, it m be said, were the weakest part of the whole scheme.

Not so with Robert Cromie's great Gaumont Pal (now the Odeon), Hammersmith, which, it was claim was the 'last word in modern architecture' at the oper in March 1932. This cinema, situated on one of the m prominent suburban sites in London, was conditio very largely by the shape and size of its site. The corne

architect's original sketch of the
ior. Architect: George Cole

ham Palace Road and Queen Street presented the
itect with that most difficult of all architectural prob-
s, running a building round a corner yet retaining
y in the total façade as well as in the frontage show-
on side streets. Cromie decided on the grand gesture
made the vast frontage—190 feet wide with nine
ances—sweep round the corner in a bold segmental
e stopped by two brick pavilions at each end. It
ted a dramatic and monumental effect. The façade
f was finished in red brick and a white cast stone.

Behind the colonnaded front to the first floor the Tea-room
extended the full length of the entrance, about 83 feet
overall.

The site in this case clearly dictated the final plan shape—
it was symmetrical and fan-shaped in outline with all the
side walls radiating from a centre-point behind the stage.
The cross walls were all curved parallel to the main elevation
wall. The advantages of the fan-shaped plan were clearly
indicated in this example. The width at the rear of the
auditorium was nearly 170 feet converging towards a

119

At the console of a 1930's cinema organ

proscenium of 64 feet, thus focussing attention directly on to the screen. It also created an impression of spaciousness that was not in the least diminished by the vast cantilevered balcony, which held 2,000 people.

The opening films shown at the Gaumont were the comedy *A Night Like This* starring Tom Walls, Ralph Lynn and Winifred Shotter, and the thriller *Bad Company* with Helen Twelvetrees and Ricardo Cortez. On the stage an *Easter Egg Review* was presented with eighty performers, including the luscious Gaumont Girls. The Gaumont Palace Symphony Orchestra conducted by de Groot ('*he is never highbrow, but he is always uplifting*') made certain that the musical feast was to everyone's taste. At the Compton organ sat Mr Leslie James with a varied programme and a technique that brought out the organ's 'double touch'.

The theatre organ itself was a mighty electrical beast with four manuals, nearly 200 stop keys and 60 thumb and toe pistons. It was claimed (inevitably) that it could imitate every instrument in the modern orchestra. The unit organ had become a favourite feature of the cinema show by this time and each new super-de-luxe competed for the services of the finest players and the most elaborate instruments. The 'Reginalds' of this world—Fortt, Dixon, Porter-Brown, seated at the consoles of their respective Compton, Conacher

or mighty Wurlitzer, captivated their audiences by sh virtuoso performances. The rise of the cinema organist responsible for the employment, somewhat later, amateurs whose excessive use of the 'wobble' tremul not only annoyed the audience but eventually brought instrument into disrepute. This sort of playing was countered in many of the smaller 'supers' throughout country where the metropolitan organist's skill was imita —including his entry and exit from the bowels of orchestra pit on a rising platform—but was neither matc nor paid for.

The unit organ itself was the cheapest and most versa available substitute for the orchestra that had been a feat of the cinema in silent days. It had the power to simu the whole orchestra during intervals or it could be subd to provide suitable accompaniment for the silent comed that still formed part of the programme after the introduc of talkies. The instrument suffered at first because peo confused it with the traditional church organ which, though it can also imitate a number of instruments in orchestra, is by no means an electrical 'orchestral unit the same type. Some idea of the size and cost of these u —including console, elevator and chambers—can be from the Wurlitzer 'Wizard' at the Trocadero which £15,000 and weighed 15 tons, while other cinemas insta the British Compton unit for about £10,000. A really organ required 100 miles of wiring.

The positioning of the organ console and the grille the organ chambers was usually left to the architec interior designer and experiments were made with organ housing over the proscenium (Regal, Birkenh or more commonly within the splayed walls to the p scenium (Trocadero, Davis' and so on).

The bigger the cinema the more ambitious the second equipment became and at the beginning of the thir nearly all the mammoth super-de-luxe houses had full s facilities as well as the giant organ. George Coles's Gaum State at Kilburn (1937) clearly outshone anything that been built before. It was described at the time as his 'crowning achievement' and indeed it was. It was a g by any standard, comparable only in Europe with Bell Gaumont Palace in Paris. Built at a cost of approxima £350,000 it provided seating accommodation for 4,00

Architecturally it was (and for that matter still i truncated cream and black faience skyscraper with n

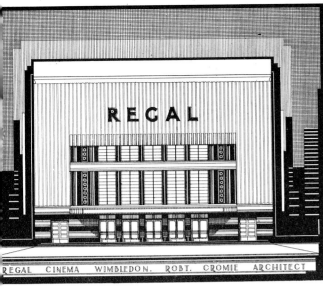

REGAL CINEMA WIMBLEDON. ROBT. CROMIE ARCHITECT

The Regal (now Odeon),
Wimbledon. Architect: Robert
Cromie

Joseph Gomersall, the Manchester cinema designer

slits up the sides and two smaller towers flanking the main feature. Internally the auditorium bears a strong resemblance to the Trocadero, with a wide sweeping balcony and long vertical niches each pinpointed by hanging ornamental lamps. The American-modern exterior gives little indication of the continued desire for a Renaissance interior. The pre-auditorium space and generous backstage spaces are the main feature of the carefully worked out plan. With the main axis of the building lying parallel to the road the architect had to devise a route from the main foyer on the High Road to the back of the main stalls and to the circle. Cleverly, the ninety-degree change of direction occurred at the point of the elliptical marble staircase hall, which acted as the focus of the plan and the visual pivot of the whole design. Everyone entering the building went through this hall and then into the succeeding apartments. With 4,000 people inside the auditorium it was also possible to accommodate another 4,000 in the waiting spaces.

The Provincial 'Supers'

Not all the cinemas of the super era were large record-breaking buildings. The hard core of the work going on in architects' offices throughout the country was for the smaller, luxurious—often 'modernistic'—palace. Some of these buildings were admirable answers to the problem of creating an acceptable environment for an optimum-sized audience of between 1,400 and 1,800 persons.

A E Shennan, a Liverpool architect who later bec. Lord Mayor of the City, was a confident cinema desig. Of his work the Mayfair, set in a populous suburb of city, is a good example of the medium-sized luxury ho. This same confidence can be seen in the work of the Lon. architect Robert Cromie, who built cinemas for m. circuits and whose medium-sized buildings were alw. designed with individuality and a certain amount. *panache*. The Regal (now the Odeon), Wimbledon, and Ritz, Birkenhead, have stood the test of time and English weather extremely well. His small Paris Cinem. Regent Street, opened in 1939, was particularly fine with auditorium relying entirely on the freely curved walls. ceiling—with integral concealed lighting—to create interesting and acoustically excellent space. Cromie responsible for the erection of over fifty cinema buildi. between 1928 and 1940.

The Manchester firm of Drury and Gomersall w. responsible for a number of major provincial cinemas in north of England during the boom years. They were typ. of the smaller office organised to prepare schemes picture theatres at speed and competitively. With a sr. staff they completed two or three major schemes each y.

Joseph Gomersall, who ran the practice, was a pers. able and handsome young man in the days of the cine. boom. He travelled widely and picked up ideas on continent that greatly influenced the work that was un. way in his office. Like many of his contemporaries he ha. background of work in theatre building and restorat. and with his partner, Drury (who did not in fact work. the Manchester office), he quickly established a reputat. as a specialist in building construction. Drury, in fact, came well known throughout the country for his textbo. on construction produced in collaboration with Jaggar.

The Regent Picture Theatre, Fallowfield (1929), first 'super' cinema produced by the firm, was decora. in the Spanish style. The frontage was comparatively pla. painted white and with a colonnaded verandah above main entrance doors. At night the flood-lighting lit up whole of the exterior and brought out in sharp relief effects of the canopy and the arch in the long auditori. wall. The interior was decorated in keeping with its. ternal Spanish character with a wall treatment in roug. textured plaster, an idea copied directly from Americ. domestic interior design. In the Souvenir Program.

uced for the opening night in August 1929 the
agement showed that they were aware of the growing
est in talkies, providing 'facilities for the immediate
llation of the same should patrons desire Sound Films.
felt, however, that it will be better to provide a first-
Orchestra and the best Silent Films obtainable to
mence with and to obtain later the opinion of Patrons
whether Talking Films are desired or not'. This was
ntiment expressed by many of the provincial and out-
own-centre circuits at that time, who felt the talkies
little more than a passing novelty.

rury and Gomersall were after 'original' cinemas, and
ng any inspiration from known foreign sources the
sic tome, Banister Fletcher's *History of Architecture on*

the Comparative Method, was available on the architects'
bookshelf for consultation. It was a comprehensive book
that could provide details for almost every style imaginable.
Certainly it was to Banister Fletcher's book that the
architects turned for inspiration for the Neo-Egyptian
'Pyramid' at Sale. Here the exterior was fashioned into the
form of a pylon—with windows added—and above the
entrance doors four columns with hybrid Bell-type capitals
carried the neon lettering and the central clock. Inside, the
hypostyle auditorium was decorated in Egyptian style in
fibrous plaster. Even the origin did not escape the desire
for stylistic unity and this was decorated with images of
Pharaoh's slaves. The consistency of the detailing was
remarkable: papyrus and lotus flower forms ran up the

Regent Picture Theatre,
wfield, Manchester.
itects: Drury and Gomersall

The Pyramid (Odeon), Sale,
Cheshire. The front elevation

Left At work assembling the
Egyptian style organ console

interior of the Pyramid

The Regal Super Cinema,
Altrincham, Cheshire.
Architects: Drury and Gomersall

e of the proscenium arch, while above the centre of the
ge area a winged solar disc spread out its arms as a symbol
protection—presumably of the new-found affluence of
 cinema exhibitor.

Drury and Gomersall were also the architects for what
s described by the promoters as *the* 'Super Cinema in
 Suburbs'. In 1931 the Regal, Altrincham—designed to
'A CATHEDRAL OF CINEMAS' (shades of Roxy
e)—was planted in Manchester's wealthiest and heal-
est suburb, with 'a commanding and delightful Terra
tta frontage . . . majestic and imposing . . . that always

retains its "seaside" appearance'. Seaside? Another virtue
appears to have been its cleanliness, and the blurb continued, 'it can be washed down'.

From the planning point of view this cinema had a number of original features, and of course, as with all the work
from the Drury and Gomersall office, it was extremely
well constructed and logically planned. The whole building
was steel framed—over 200 tons of steel were used—the
roof itself being supported by 90-foot long principal girders
and the balcony supported by one large girder, 90 feet long
and 14 feet deep and weighing 50 tons. The total cost of the

building was in the region of £27,000, about the average price for a suburban cinema at the time.

The general colour scheme within the auditorium followed the 'luxurious' pattern, and silver and gold predominated. The inside of the dome in the ceiling of the auditorium gave the impression of being decorated in beaten silver even though in reality it was carried out in plastic paint treated with a metallic finish. The art of the interior decorator was matched by the ingenuity of the electrical engineer in this as in many other cinema buildings, and the use of concealed coloured lighting heightened the total effect.

In this super cinema nothing was spared. For the discriminating audience that the management hoped to entice to its shows, films were booked well in advance, advertised, and programmes were changed every week ('in order that the best of the available "Super Productions" could be shown'). An orchestra was provided (because 'music built up the cinema business'), British Thomson-Houston talking equipment was installed (because it was British), a Compton organ was included (for the same reason) and a large café (in the British rather than the French style) was also provided. The comfort of the patron was also taken into careful consideration: draught screens were erected around all entrances, a confectionery kiosk was provided inside the waiting-lounge, five exits were provided from the balcony and circle, and a car park was situated behind the building.

126

This same concern for quality and comfort can be in the planning of other super cinemas by this fir Moston, Banbury and Sale Moor, and in the highly suc ful Carlton (now Essoldo) Cinema situated near the c of Stockport.

The Odeons

The Odeon Organisation more than any other circu the 1930s established a distinctive style of cinema des

The Odeon circuit itself became part of J Arthur R great empire after the death of its founder, Oscar Deu in 1941. Since then the Odeon Organisation has be the largest of all the main cinema groups in Britain.

Oscar Deutsch had dictated the sort of 'image buildings were to have. They took their name—a Nickel-odeons had done much earlier—from the G The Odeion of Pericles, built on the slopes of the Acro is given as the definitive source. Its first twentieth-cer namesake was at Perry Barr, Birmingham, in 1930. I considerably less Grecian than its name implied; it positively Moorish. Oddly enough it was the letterir the main facade that really evoked the Attic origins c cinema name. Pearce Signs, a well-known London fir neon-light manufacturers, created and used for the time at Perry Barr the characteristic Odeon symbol—a sign with large individual letters silhouetted against illuminated background.

and night views of the
lton (now the Essoldo)
ema, Stockport. Architects:
ry and Gomersall

te **The Odeon Theatre,**
tanding and below
ect's **working drawing**
:ect: **Harry Weedon**

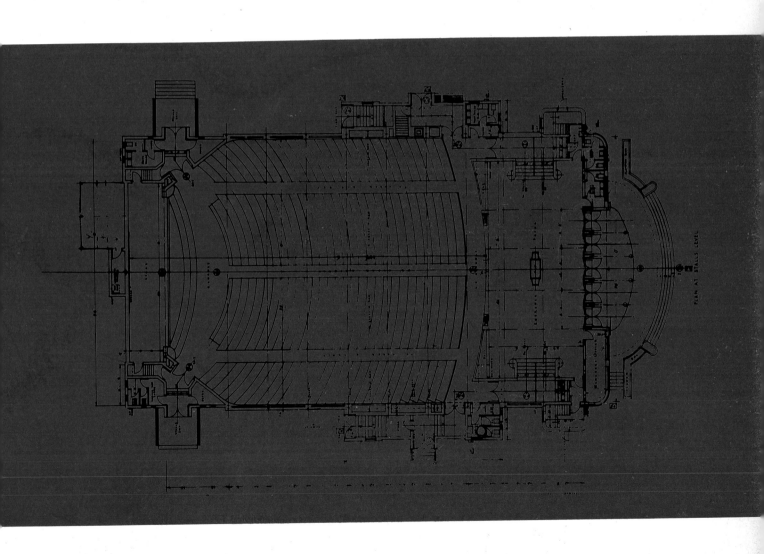

The Odeon Theatre, York, 1936
Opposite **The architect's working
drawings showing ground and
balcony plans.
Architect: Harry Weedon**

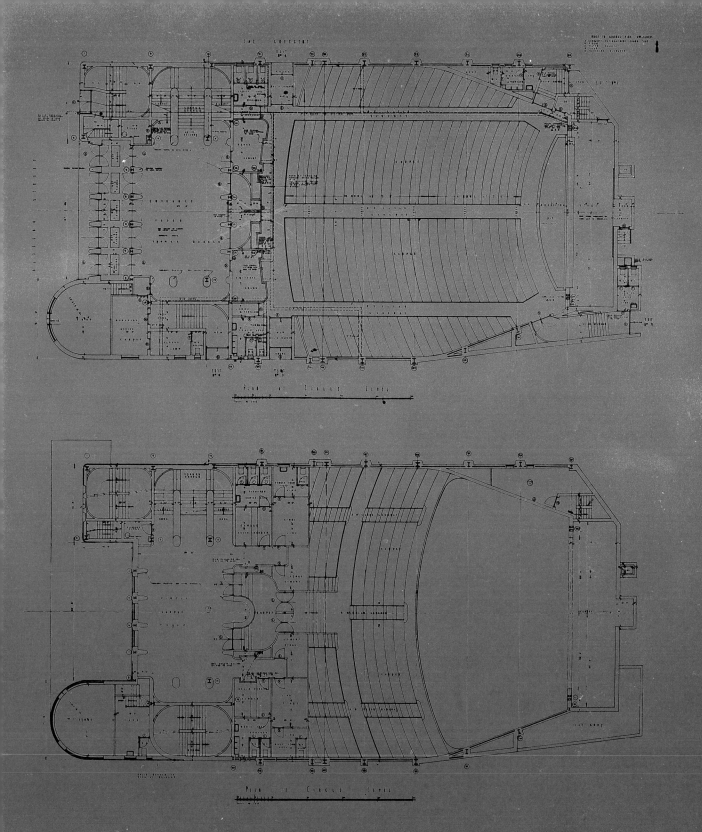

The Odeon Theatre, Colwyn Bay,
1936. Right **Ground floor plan.**
Architect: Harry Weedon

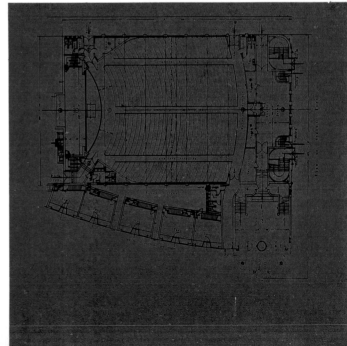

Odeon Theatre, Scarborough,
6. Architect: Harry Weedon

site **The Odeon Theatre,**
on Coldfield, 1936.
itect: Harry Weedon

architect's perspective of the
on Theatre, Scarborough,
. Architect: Harry Weedon

Above **The Odeon Theatre, Dudley,**
1937. Interior of auditorium (top)
and main frontage.
Architect: Harry Weedon

135

Odeon Theatre, Morecombe, 1937
Opposite **The architect's working
drawing for the ground floor.
Architect: Harry Weedon**

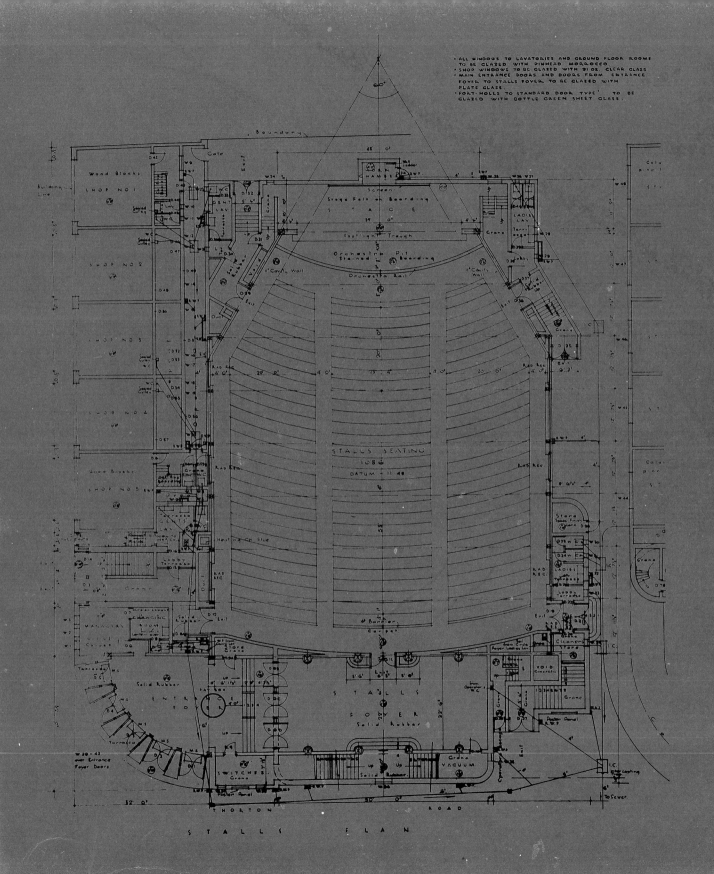

The architect's perspective
drawing showing proposals for
the Odeon Theatre, Chester, 1936

Opposite The Odeon Theatre,
Lancaster, 1936. Architect:
Harry Weedon

The Odeon circuit had been established in 1933, but Deutsch had already made his mark in the film exhibiting business before the opening of his first Odeon. The son of an industrialist, he was born in Birmingham in 1893. After a brief period in the family firm he was persuaded by a group of Birmingham businessmen to enter the expanding film industry. He became chairman of Victory Motion Pictures, a Midlands group, who were acting as agents for one of the major film distributing companies in England. He soon saw the limitations of renting out films and became the owner of the Crown Cinema, Coventry, in 1925.

Oscar Deutsch also made his own position on the design

The Odeon, Chingford.
Architect: Andrew Mather

of cinemas clear. He wrote, in the supplement on Cine[mas] and Theatres that appeared in *Design and Construction* March 1937: 'it was always my ambition to have build[ings] which were individual and striking, but which were alw[ays] objects of architectural beauty . . . we endeavour to m[ake] our buildings express the fact that they are specially ere[cted] as the homes of the latest, most progressive entertainm[ent] in the world today . . .' Many of the designs for the [new] Odeons were influenced by Mrs Deutsch, who acted as [a] consultant for the interior decoration. She had advised [on] the textures and colours for the interior of the Perry [Bar] Odeon and later became a director of the Odeon subsidi[ary] Decorative Crafts Ltd. In her designs she gauged the so[cial] conditions and atmosphere of a particular locality [and] planned her decorations accordingly. Spacious, g[ood] coloured interiors—'in impeccable taste'—were conside[red] appropriate at Hampstead, Haverstock Hill and at Ches[ter] while at the 'old and historic' town of Faversham the w[alls] of the auditorium, somewhat predictably, were decora[ted] in half-timbering.

Generally the new Odeons were distinguished extern[ally] by the use of square panels of cream faience tiling an[d a] single tower feature. Only where local conditions—or Lo[cal] Authorities—demanded a different solution was this ele[va]tional treatment changed. The Odeons designed by Ha[rry] W Weedon at York and Chester were both treated [as] massive brickwork boxes.

The use of large areas of tiling, unrelieved except b[y a] few windows, meant that it was possible for the desig[ner] to use the whole bulk of his building to create a dram[atic] effect without resorting to decorative detailing or pseu[do] period motifs.

Deutsch's cinema interests soon began to expand in [the] Midlands and by 1931 he had six cinemas under his cont[rol.] By the time Odeon Theatres Ltd was formed in Octo[ber] 1933 he had the eighth largest circuit in Britain. Four y[ears] later the County Group of cinemas came under the con[trol] of Odeon. In 1938 the first-run Paramount Theatres w[ere] taken over by Odeon, and the Astorias at Brixton, Streath[am,] Finsbury Park and the Old Kent Road, as well as the la[rge] Paramounts in Manchester, Leeds and Newcastle, [all] became part of the stock.

With the Odeons Oscar Deutsch created a new bran[d of] cinema. He established a policy of acquiring sites for [new] cinemas in strategic areas—usually areas where new hous[ing]

A preliminary sketch by the architect, Cecil Howitt, for an Odeon

The Odeon, Bournemouth

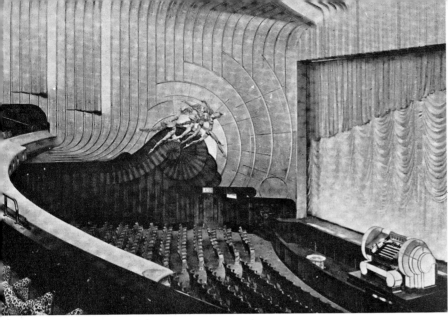

The coal black Odeon, Leicester Square, London. Architects: Andrew Mather and Harry Weedon. The architects' drawing of the main facade, the interior (recently altered) and a night view. The interior was of ribbed plaster for acoustic reasons

development was about to take place— and to his great credit he stimulated the building industry at a time when the effects of the Depression were still being felt. His success, it seems, knew no bounds and at the time of the public issue of shares in 1937 the Odeon circuit owned 300 cinemas and was worth six million pounds.

From his Birmingham office in the early years of the Odeon organisation Deutsch carried out a programme of acquiring sites and building new cinemas throughout the country. In charge of all the design work was the Birmingham architect Harry W Weedon, a private practitioner, whose buildings can still be seen in towns throughout the country. Weedon acted for his clients in an exclusive capacity, not only designing new cinema buildings and reconstructing old ones but also vetting the designs of other leading architects employed on Odeon projects. Among these were Cecil Howitt of Nottingham and the London architects Andrew Mather and George Coles, Yates, Cook and Derbyshire, and T P Bennett and Son.

Harry Weedon's Birmingham office was probably the best organised of all architects' offices in this country for the uninterrupted process of mass-producing cinemas during the boom years. The method of working was efficient enough to cope with an endless stream of new commissions. A comprehensive design brief was prepared by Weedon in conjunction with the Odeon 'Theatres' Technical Department. This gave to the assistants working on individual schemes technical information on seating spacing, sanitary accommodation standards, projection room layout and equipment, acoustics, heating and ventilating, floor finishes, canopy designs and so on. A chart was prepared in the office, incorporating Home Office as well as LCC regulations, showing six possible arrangements of auditorium seating from the type with a single centre block and side aisles to the more elaborate layout of four blocks of seats with three intermediate gangways. The chart also included varying numbers of rows of seats and gave the total seating per block at a glance. General details were also prepared in the office for joinery, barriers, rester rails, horn chambers, lighting troughs etc. These were all subject to minor alterations in individual projects due to the slightly different requirements of certain local authorities.

Weedon introduced specially designed boxwood scales for the use of his assistants, giving standard stair treads and risers to suit the regulations. On these scales back-to-back seating and seat width dimensions of 1 foot 8 inches were also included.

The effect of such office organisation—probably only paralleled in this country by the office of Sir John Burnett, Tait and Lorne—did not lead to dull, uninteresting buildings or to what the critics have called duplicated house-styling. In fact, it led to the design of a number of extremely efficient and quite distinctive buildings. With the Odeon work in Weedon's office the only concession made to house-styling was confined to the use of the vertical 'tower' feature, the use of standard titles and the employment of a faience or panel type of external cladding. Therefore there is a certain similarity of treatment about all the Odeons of the 'thirties, but the varying factors involved in each design —siting, overall size, the proximity or otherwise of neighbouring buildings and the regulations concerning display and planning—made a consistency of treatment impossible of the type attained by the UFA circuit in Germany. One has only to compare three of Weedon's buildings at Crewe, Chester and Dudley to see the diversity that could be obtained within the framework of design just mentioned.

Andrew Mather and Harry Weedon jointly provided the design for the *chef-d'œuvre* of Deutsch's organisation, the Leicester Square Odeon. This black granite building was built on the site of the old Alhambra Theatre and opened its doors to the public in 1937. Surmounted by a slim tower feature 120 feet high rising from a 100-foot wide frontage, the building covers an area of 27,000 square feet. At the

back is a 10-storey office block. The exterior of the buil[ding] appropriately enough in the entertainment centre o[f] country, was designed for the then largest display of [illu]minated advertising in the world. When the anony[mous] façade recedes at night into the darkness and the lig[ht] panels and titles stand out it appears that the old Ge[rman] concept of 'night architecture' has been taken to its lo[gical] conclusion. Internally the bright spacious auditorium [seats] 2,300 seats, a thousand of which are accommodated o[n an] unusual raked balcony. The treatment of this interior s[pace] is carried out by a series of fibrous plaster 'waves' [which] conceal lighting coves and blend with the large semi-c[ircle] above the square proscenium arch.

Harry Weedon, the Bermingham Cinema architect

Search for Style

'super' cinema automatically became associated with [mod]ernistic' expression in architecture. Although few [exam]ples can be numbered among the more significant [buil]dings of the true Modern Movement, at least they pre-[pare]d the ground for the acceptance of modern ideas in [this] country in the postwar decades.

[W]ith the concern for modernity came also a desire for [origi]nality and for the consistent treatment of the total [struc]ture. The massing of the building became more impor-[tant] than the 'tarting-up' of pseudo-Classical façades. [Orig]inality of façade treatment ranged from the carefully [cont]rolled flat exterior of Robert Cromie's Regal, Wimble-[don] to the extrovert elevations of Andrew Mather's [Lon]gford Odeon or Henry Elder's cash register front for [the L]ongford (Essoldo), Stretford (c. 1938). Odd stylistic [perv]ersions still continued to appear—usually when the [arch]itect had to deal with a difficult setting—and sadly [thes]e buildings were erected in our more historic and [envi]ronmentally valuable towns.

[M]ather's Odeon at Faversham could not have been more [ap]propriate, while the Tudor, West Kirby (in Cheshire ['bla]ck and white'), the Embassy, Esher, and Cromie's [Rega]l, Godalming (with elevations approved by Sir Edwin [Lut]yens) are unfortunate attempts to disguise the true [natu]re of cinema architecture. A cinema building cannot [be c]ompromised and disguised to look like a medieval town [hous]e, a block of flats or the *Petit Trianon*. Occasionally [the] mock tudor style did come off as in W E Trent's [Gau]mont, Salisbury, but in this case the original frontage, [repu]tedly by Pugin, was incorporated as part of the design [and] the Gothicky world of the interior recalled the previous [use] of the building by John Halle, a wealthy medieval wool [mer]chant in the city.

[T]rent's other work for Provincial Cinematograph [The]atres and Gaumont-British was more in the modernistic [veni]t. His finest building was the early 'super' cinema [opp]osite Victoria Station called the New Victoria. Opened [in 1]930 it was quite different from any other English ex-[amp]le at that time. It was in line with current Continental [prac]tice. Sympathetic to its surroundings, it made a fitting [cont]ribution to the existing street architecture with two [iden]titive façades on parallel streets. Internally it was [desi]gned with an impressive although considerably over-[deco]rated interior. The work on the interior, carried out in

conjunction with E Walmsley Lewis, was distinctly Germanic in feeling. The theme was an underwater palace with sea colours on the walls and hanging shell-like light fittings reminiscent of the stalactite forms of Hans Poelzig's *Grosses Schauspielhaus* interior of 1919. The curved and banded exterior still suggests a closer affinity to the work of Erich Mendelsohn and the more conservative Functiona-list architects of a slightly later period. But it was a typical English exterior in that it was designed as an 'image' sym-bolic of a cinema and not a clear expression of the interior arrangement. This criticism is not to denigrate the building as a whole, which has proved to be one of the most popular and comfortable cinemas in London, rather it goes to show

**The Longford (Essoldo) Cinema,
Stretford, Manchester.
Architect: Henry Elder**

The New Victoria, London.
The main front and interiors.
Architect: W. E. Trent

control; the patron moved from space to space with ease before finally approaching the large symmetrically placed auditorium. Once inside this space, seating over 2,000 people, the curved fan shape became apparent. The auditorium itself had excellent sight lines and full stage facilities—a luxury that most of the major circuits had done away with years before.

In the important Warner Theatre, Leicester Square, opened in 1938 on the site of Daly's old theatre, the stage had been reduced to a twelve-foot wide passageway behind the screen. The Warner, designed by E A Stone in association with T R Somerford, was a movie building pure and simple. It possessed all the very latest innovations in acoustical control, internal lighting, external advertising, paybox design and pre-auditorium comfort. From a planning point of view it differed little from some of Stone's earlier buildings but in its muted decorative treatment and size (only 1,775 seats even in Leicester Square) it proved to be a new type of building altogether. Externally it could not have been more different from the black-faced Odeon a few yards away and clearly it represents the other side of the exhibitors' coin, the American inspired, extrovert structure that combines a day and a night façade both of which stress the flashiness and symbolism surrounding the cinema.

The Curzon, Mayfair

Without any doubt, the most aesthetically satisfying, comfortable and indeed the most functional cinema in this country during the 'thirties was the Curzon, Mayfair, designed by Sir John Burnet, Tait and Lorne and opened in 1934. It was small compared with most other super cinemas, seating only 500 people. In a contemporary report in *The Architect and Building News* a writer welcomed it as a departure from the 'heavily balconied auditorium and Hispano-Hollywood atmosphere' of so many supers. The cinema audience, the writer goes on, will 'exchange a cathedral for a chapel-of-ease, and will be able at long last to enjoy films under almost ideal conditions'.

The Curzon was the first of the small luxury theatres designed to show films that were 'not acceptable to the big West-End theatres on account of their limited appeal'. Appropriately enough, in its Mayfair setting, it was a remarkably refined building, simple in outline and beautifully detailed. The elevational treatment was derived direct-

t it was not always possible to get all the various parts of building together to appear as a cohesive design. The hitect had done well in providing many interesting pre-ditorium levels and spaces and also an auditorium of rly 3,000 seats on such a restricted site.

Trent's buildings were all marked by a notably compact n which in many cases overcame the problems of an kward site. His work is amongst the best produced for er cinemas anywhere and when he did have the portunity of designing for an open site his planning skill s matched by confident elevational treatment.

With the Gaumont Palace, Wolverhampton (1932), he opted a façade treatment similar to the New Victoria t was able to sweep his low banded elevation around the rner in a wide curve. At Finchley, his Gaumont (1938) ilt on an island site was even more successful externally. e tall semi-circular corner 'feature' joined a long hori-ntal area of brickwork and under this an elegant canopy otected the entrance doors. Inside, everything was under

The Gaumont, Finchley

Opposite **The old Curzon Cinema, Mayfair, London**

ly from the work of the Dutch Master, Willem Marinus Dudok, and had a distinct sympathy to that architect's Hilversum Town Hall. Externally the building was faced with dark grey and red bricks with stone dressings. Outside advertising and signs were kept to the absolute minimum. Internally the auditorium was a simple single-storey space, focused directly on to a large screen and entirely free from superficial decoration. The suspended ceiling was coved and its curves joined the auditorium walls to create a completely integrated interior. The walls and ceiling were rose-tinted, the pullman-type seats finished in a deep blue upholstery, and the exit doors painted scarlet. The stark simplicity of the interior relied for its effect on the three-colour lighting system concealed in the five curved sconces spanning the ceiling. During each performance the lights were dimmed to the required level of 'morality' lighting. The entrance foyer was also treated in a simple uncluttered way but was remarkably small for the size of the auditorium. Above this vestibule the offices of the manager (the Marquis

148

of Casa Maury) and the projection suite were situated

It would be unfair to give the impression that just cause the old Curzon received the approbation of mod architects it was the last word in cinema perfection for layman. This it certainly was not. Although everyone visited the building commented on its comfort, to son was too stark, and one well-known film critic has recor that the first time he went into the Curzon they were show a film of underwater swimming and he had the immed impression of being caught in a gigantic goldfish b Architects, it seems, cannot please everyone! No doub this case the architects had pleased their client. It was fit therefore that they were appointed to design the Curzon (completed in 1966) which is situated on the s site although now it is only the lower part of an office bu ing. The two Curzons in their respective ways express difference there is between the era of the complete su luxury building of the 'thirties and the integrated cin of the present day.

The interior of the o[ld]
Curzon. This cinema [has]
been replaced by the
new Curzon,
see pages 196–7

**Continental cinemas
and the 'functional'
design solution**

Consistency of architectural treatment, and efficient and interesting plans as well as sophisticated modes of decoration, were the prerogative of the Continental cinema designers. Generally their buildings were much smaller than American and English examples.

On the whole, British cinema architects—like their clients—had little interest in aesthetics. They showed even less interest in trying to come to terms with the 'new architecture' that was being advocated and demonstrated by their Continental colleagues. There was, of course, in the work of English designers 'a natural development'—as one notable cinema architect has put it—due to technical advances, but this did not always result in an enhanced architectural form. Indeed, it is amazing that any good results were achieved at all under the conditions that prevailed in this country during the boom years. The field was competitive, regulations were stringent and the demand for buildings was seemingly insatiable. Harry Weedon, who contributed more to a distinct type of cinema design than any other architect in this country, claims to have had over sixty schemes on the drawing board at one time, all in various stages of design or construction. With this sort of demand it becomes impossible to develop a design fully.

In the light of such facts it is not surprising that the marked difference between English and Continental cinemas is essentially one of architectural quality.

As early as 1922, Gunnar Asplund, a noted Swedish 'Modern Romantic' architect, designed the Skandia Cine-ma in Stockholm which set an extremely high standar[d] design and decoration. At the time it was called 'the [most] beautiful cinema building in the world'. Relying on sim[ple] decorative treatment and a cleverly devised plan the ar[chi]tect was clearly convinced that a cinema was not merel[y an] extension of conventional theatre design. He did, howe[ver] make some basic mistakes. There were serious defect[s in] the design of the sight lines, and the seats were unspr[ung] and decidedly uncomfortable. Even so the popularit[y of] this cinema with Swedish audiences indicates that the [de]lightful semi-atmospheric interior with the restrained c[las]sical detailing of its auditorium outweighed any [more] obvious limitations. It was certainly the most original [and] sophisticated cinema of its day.

It was left to the Germans to develop a truly functi[onal] cinema architecture. They were aided in this by cer[tain] planning requirements based on distinctive national c[on]ventions common to all entertainment buildings in [that] country. Chief of these was the desire to extend cine[ma] design along the lines of the numerous small opera ho[uses] that existed in most German towns of any size. A charac[ter]istic of these buildings was the use of wide gangways [en]circling the auditorium for promenading, and the p[ro]vision of large-scale cloakrooms but few foyer or vestib[ule] spaces. This meant architecturally that the auditor[ium] could be an independent element in the design, tre[ated] freely and shaped according to the needs of the site and [the] requirements of good vision.

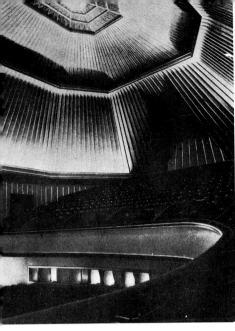

The Capitol, Berlin. Interior and main front.
Architect: Hans Poelzig

Opposite **An elevational drawing
of the Piccadilly Theatre, Berlin.
Architect: Fritz Wilms**

Paul Zucker's book *Theater und Lichtpielhäuser* (Berlin, 1926) gives a good summary of the attitude of German designers to the problem of cinema design over the fourteen years 1912–1926. It is by no means an exhaustive study but the examples that are shown indicate significant changes, both in plan and elevational treatment, and in the evolution of the cinema as a building type. The German *Kino* gradually assumed a distinctive form and an aesthetic quality peculiarly its own. The first attempts were typically Germanic—solid, heavy façades, still very much in the theatre idiom and lacking the sophistication of later examples such as Hans Poelzig's fine Berlin Capitol of 1926. The Union-Palast in Berlin, designed by E Simon in 1912, was externally a Neo-Classic monster. It had an ill-proportioned entablature sitting uncomfortably on a number of columns let into part of the façade. The plan was simply a box within a box. At the back the flat balcony spanned between the main walls and underneath this was the foyer space. Situated adjacent to the foyer were the entrance hall and staircase. All access points to the auditorium on the ground floor were off a promenade that ran down the right-hand side of the building, while the stage was a simple opening in the proscenium wall in front of which was a small orchestra pit. At the front stood a screen.

Hugo Pal's Marmorhaus, also in Berlin and built about the same date, was a much more elaborate affair in plan with a direct entrance from the street leading to two staircase towers which gave access to the auditorium. The flat

stalls area was again enclosed by a simple rectangular but above this a horseshoe-shaped balcony covered m of the stalls.

Neither of these cinemas had the power or interest of slightly earlier examples in Berlin and in Dresden. O Kaufmann's Cines on the Nollendorfplatz in Berlin, b in 1911, was a mature building by any standard. It reflec in its elevations the simplicity of the new movie techniqu A rectangular stone building, it presented blank walls three street frontages only broken up on the main façade an ornamental entrance loggia. This single-storey h domed entrance was surmounted by a Buddha-like sta and recessed into the concave curved front wall. The p was completely symmetrical. Inside the auditorium floors of the stalls and the balcony were raked, and an tremely interesting feature was the use of a prominent pub staircase from the lower stalls to the front of the balco the line of the staircase rising out of the base of the au torium was then continued across the balcony as a s handrail. This unusual design idea for the interior of cinema gave a unity that is often lost when balcony a stalls are rigidly segregated.

The Union-Theater, Dresden, designed by Mar Pietszch in 1911, was a thorough-going attempt to prov audiences with a building appropriate to its purpose. egg-shaped auditorium was indeed prophetic of the v many designers would try to give a sense of intimacy and closure in their buildings some twenty or thirty years lat

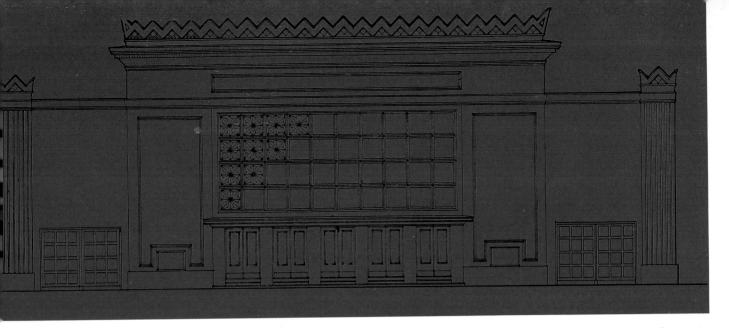

apparently Pietszch was not conditioned in his design by
as much as by the need of the spectator to be well posi-
ed within the auditorium and to be reasonably close to
creen. At this early stage acoustics had little part to play
e design. The resultant effect for its date is remarkable;
only did the curved interior have a basic unity but the
ony, arranged as a number of boxes between columns,
f served to give the interior a dignified appearance.

mediately after the First World War the German film
stry was reorganised to cope with the demand for new
s and cinemas. After an initial period of frustration,
tages and delays in the building industry, new cinemas
e erected that left the embryonic ideas of the pre-war
od far behind.

he UFA Company which went through a difficult phase
e 'twenties commissioned Fritz Wilms to design a
ber of their cinemas after 1924. His work, which had a
acteristic simplicity, obviously owed much to Oscar
fmann. There was however a distinct difference in the
earance of buildings in the post-war period when a new
gn factor had emerged. This was the new desire for
rtising the building interior by the use of glass areas in
façade and by external light sources. The movies were
ght-time entertainment and in their new cinema build-
German architects quickly grasped this point, making
r structures 'night buildings' with 'neutral' façades and
ninated lettering as an important part of the design.
Morton Shand in his book *Modern Theatres and Cine-*

mas (London, 1930) summed up the aims of the German
architects by claiming that their fame rested on a masterly
economy of material which obtains the greatest possible
effect with a minimum of detail, and on the fact that the
cinema façade should be little more than an unobtrusive
neutral background for neon-lighting, a masonry echo of
the linen screen. 'They argue that the cinema depends
wholly, in a technical sense, on the contrast between darkness and light; and that it has no concern with daylight
effects. The cinema sleeps by day as other buildings do by
night.'

Fritz Wilm's Piccadilly in Berlin was a building that took
into consideration this new factor of 'night architecture'
with a large yet simple rectangular screen-shaped window
that could be lit up externally. It still retained a traditional
dignity of façade and unlike so many later examples—on the
Continent and in Britain—it did not sacrifice architectural
distinction for the sake of producing an artificial lighting
effect.

Max Taut's study for a *Kino Palast* (1920) on a site in
Berlin remained a paper project. But the drawings show how
this architect struggled with the problems of the external
form of the building until a unified and consistent design
emerged. The result is a good example of the modern functional cinema building with advertising, entrance and
glazed surrounding spaces clearly expressed.

Some clear difference must be made between those cinemas that were merely a product of a commercial situation

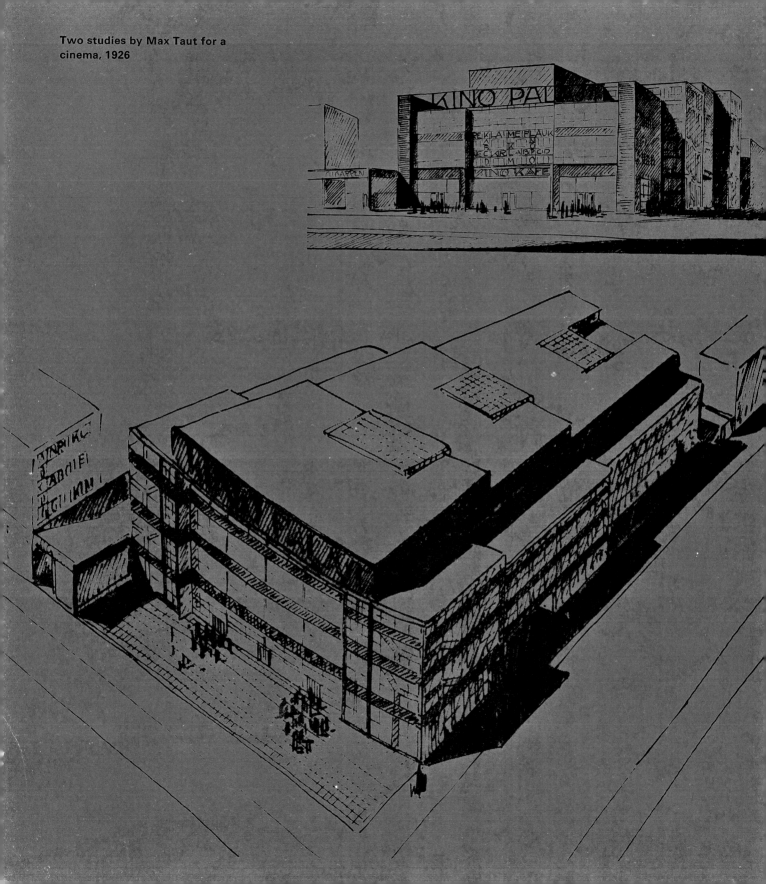

Two studies by Max Taut for a
cinema, 1926

buildings that were produced by architects intent on [produc]ing a truly modern functional architecture. Un[doub]tedly the finest of the modern idiom cinemas was [Eric]h Mendelsohn's Universum (Luxor Palast) built off the [fashi]onable Kurfürstendamm in Berlin during 1926–29. As [Men]delsohn's biographer Arnold Whittick has written, it is [the f]irst cinema which really 'shows the complete organic [unit]y of the whole'. Its horseshoe-shaped auditorium was [the m]ain unifying factor. The external form of the building [echo]ed this in the bold sweep of the entrance front and in [the l]ong, low, spreading roof. Inside, no atmospheric or [any] stylistic decoration distracted the attention of the au[dien]ce and each seat in the long, curved, plain auditorium [had] an excellent view of the screen. All lines in the interior [in]cluding the lighting—converged towards the screen. [T]he Universum was a machine for viewing where the [spec]tator had every comfort and must have experienced [the] all too rare pleasure of being involved in a building that [trul]y was masterful architecture. The functional require[men]ts of entry, circulation and escape were all taken care of [and] the German habit of removing one's coat before a per[form]ance began provided the architect with the opportunity [of n]eatly fitting his *Garderoben* in the promenade spaces [that] ran around the outside of the auditorium. Fourteen en[tran]ces in this surrounding wall offered free access to all [part]s of the stalls. No gangways interrupted the clear sweep [of th]e seats.

[T]he design solution that Mendelsohn provided for this cinema is so nearly perfect that it makes the work of most other architects look as though they were merely playing with the problems of circulation and decoration. It must be admitted, though, that this fine building would not have passed the British regulations for cinematograph performances!

With the success of the Universum, the UFA Company adopted the horseshoe-shaped auditorium as a standard design type and found it ideal for the new talkies. In the standard plan the seats in the main auditorium stalls stretched across the theatre while divisions were made for gangways at approximately ten-row intervals. This pattern was followed for the UFA palaces in Koblenz (1930) and Danzig (1931). In these examples the emphasis in the decoration (again a huge, long, horseshoe lighting effect) was towards the stage with a resultant symmetry at the proscenium arch.

While the Germans sought after technical efficiency and design excellence in their cinemas, the French were determined that their new Parisian theatres would be the sensation of Europe. In 1930 plans were announced for a super cinema with 6,000 seats—'*the world's biggest*' (in reality it was smaller than the Roxy). The design for this was prepared by M Belloc who was commissioned to reconstruct the existing Gaumont Palace, which had originally been formed out of the shell of the old Hippodrome situated on the Place de Clichy. The new design had a massive, cubistic façade incorporating all the latest ideas on exterior illumi-

Above and top, opposite **Erich Mendelsohn's Universum Cinema, Berlin, 1926–9**

Right **The Gaumont Palace, Paris. Architect: Henri Belloc**

Opposite, below **A good example of the stadium type of plan used in a cinema in Venice**

A modernistic frontage to a cinema in Brussels

nation. Inside, a new ground level was created, a mezzar built with 900 seats, and on top of this an upper balc constructed to hold a further 1,000 cheaper seats. The conies had no intermediate supports and rested only their ends on massive abutments which went down 100 below the structure to a solid foundation.

The Gaumont Company opened a further cinem Paris in 1931, an impressive luxury house on the Char Elysées. In plan it followed the German precedent wi small horseshoe-shaped auditorium, but instead of a si balcony it incorporated a number of galleries reaching to the gods, in the more usual Parisian music hall traditi

The décor of most French cinemas was more closely to American prototypes. Inevitably the flamboyant at spherics were popular with the average French cinemag The first atmospheric to be built in Paris was the Rex the corner of the Boulevard Poissonnière. It was erecte 1932 for Jacques Haik and designed by the French archi Bluysen in association with John Eberson. A four-thous seater, the Rex auditorium was decorated in Moroc style, with plaster villas, figures and garden ornaments ting up to silhouette against the artificial sky. It even cluded a rainbow of luminous tubes around the proscenit

After Haik's success in Paris it was not long before provinces had their own rainbow auditoria. Toulc boasted an ambitious example in 1933, and in the same the Rex was opened in Bordeaux bringing, according contemporary report, 'a note which is entirely fresh to architecture of the town'. Apart from matters of size luxury, French architects were no further in advance the design of super cinemas than their English colleagu They excelled, however, in the design of smaller news theatres and later in the new type of specialist house, so-called 'intelligentsia' cinema.

Throughout the main centres of France and the I Countries it is these specialist cinemas that still hold o interest. Neat, compact and distinctive, they brough breath of real inspiration into cinema design when it become for most architects little more than a fee-getti chore.

The Germans by this time were no longer the leader cinema design—the National Socialists had poured sc on the 'decadent' Modern Movement—and for the time England took the initiative, only to be halted by advent of war in 1939

10

Design considerations
in British cinemas
during the thirties

Three broad categories of auditorium arrangement emerged in the 'thirties: the single flat or slightly raked floor type for small cinema buildings, the stadium type with a raised tier at the rear of the auditorium, and the larger 'super' type with a single balcony. There were no similar categories of plan shape and consequently whether a cinema auditorium was fan-shaped, straight back and sides, curved or pear-shaped in plan was dependent on site factors as well as the preferences of individual designers.

If the site conditions demanded a long auditorium with a restricted width (as was the case with the Ritz, Hereford, by Leslie Kemp) or a narrow frontage (Regal, Margate, by Robert Cromie) then this very largely dictated the final plan shape. In the Ritz, Hereford, the clever planning of the pre-auditorium spaces enabled the architect to adopt a stadium plan without sacrificing any floor area by tucking the entrance foyer under the steep stalls. In Cromie's Regal the narrow frontage and deep side walls of adjoining buildings were turned to good use, with the whole of the ground floor area given over to a long entrance hall. Above this a restaurant was lit by a glass and concrete laylight. In this example the architect overcame the cramped conditions of the frontage by creating a vertical emphasis with a tower-like façade. Once through the narrow entrance hall the patron came to the spacious foyer and then to the auditorium, which was the usual size for a 1,800-seat cinema. Difficulties encountered in planning inevitably led to difficulties in construction and again it was often the ingenious rather

than the conventional structural solution that succee[...]

Modern steelwork design was used almost exclusiv[...] the construction of cinemas in this country. Great balc[...] could be carried without additional supporting col[...] obscuring the patrons' view in the back stalls, and imm[...] loads could be transferred to the wall stanchions us[...] minimum of material. As the important feature of ci[...] building from the financial point of view was 'the maxi[...] use of available space with the minimum of expenditu[...] construction' steelwork was ideal.

Reinforced concrete construction found little favo[...] could not provide the advantage of steel in either spe[...] erection, flexibility or dryness. Although a patent was [...] out for a system of dry pre-cast concrete construction [...] would have dispensed with the need to plaster interna[...] faces, this did not catch on in cinema building althou[...] was used successfully in flat construction at the time. [...] advantages offered by steel-framed and 'composite' [...] struction (brick bearing walls and steel trusses) ra[...] became obvious. It was economic, relatively easy to h[...] and fix, and it could be easily boxed in and disguised [...] fibrous plaster. In being able to span reasonable dist[...] it offered an easy solution to the problem of creating [...] areas and proscenium openings. The largest of the s[...] could be erected within twelve months.

The Kensington Cinema by Leathart and Granger[...] one of the earliest post-war steel-framed buildings in [...] the architects dissociated the main auditorium stru[...]

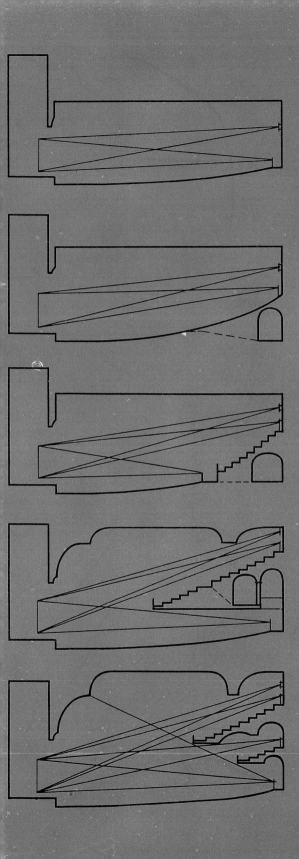

One floor type

The theatre in its simplest form, consisting of an orchestra floor only. When the lot area and good sight lines permit of the required number of seats on one floor, this type is an economical form.

Bleacher type

A variation of the one floor type, used where the depth of the auditorium requires the use of a steep gradient at the rear to secure correct sight lines.

Stadium type

A variation of the bleacher type. The seats back of the cross-over aisle are raised so that patrons using the cross-over aisle do not interfere with the line of sight. This portion of the house is steep and requires steps as in the balcony.

Single balcony type

The introduction of a balcony to secure greater seating capacity without necessarily increasing the lot area. The additional cost per seat is slight considering the results obtained.

Balcony—mezzanine type

Where the desired seating capacity of the balcony brings the balcony rail too near the proscenium arch, seats lost by reducing the length of the main balcony are obtained in a mezzanine balcony. Slight lines of rear orchestra seats are greatly improved by reducing the balcony projection.

The steel framework of the Regal,
Altrincham, Architects: Drury
and Gomersall

Below The steelwork of The
Kensington

that of the balcony. This gave the immediate advan-
⋯f being able to roof-in the building and build up the
⋯ny under satisfactory working conditions. The main
⋯and roof were constructed from arches resting on pin-
⋯gs at foundation level with wall and roof panels filling
⋯aces between the arched supports.

⋯he huge Dreamland Cinema at Margate, designed by
⋯eathart and Granger in 1935, an even more adven-
⋯s use was made of steelwork. Here it was necessary to
⋯e the auditorium across a main approach road to the
⋯ement park. The main balcony girder (which weighed
⋯s) spanned almost across the axis of the road.

⋯e block-like appearance of many English cinemas was
⋯ct result of the use of structural steel. Widths and
⋯ts of structural bays dictated the final form of build-
⋯y the division of the plan into three main elements—
⋯ce block, auditorium and stage. Another factor that
⋯sly affected the external appearance of cinema build-
⋯as the choice of a suitable shape for the roof line. The
⋯of was the first choice of most architects both for
⋯tic reasons and because it was easy and cheap to
⋯particularly after the introduction of lightweight steel
⋯ng. It was also found possible with the flat roof to step-
⋯the roof where the auditorium ceiling sloped towards
⋯oscenium and to reduce the volume—and therefore
⋯tal cost—of the building. This was done by Leathart
⋯ranger in the Sheen Cinema. The pitched roof how-
⋯ad a currency in entertainment buildings and when

finished with asbestos sheeting provided the cheapest form
of cover available. More often than not it was used by
designers with little aesthetic sensibility or on a building
that presented only its main façade to a street. On an island
or corner site its use was always visually disastrous.

To a very large extent all the foregoing factors controlled
the total shape of individual buildings. What was completely left to the imagination of the architect was the choice
of facing materials, lighting, decoration and detail planning.

With composite construction—and with the English cli-
mate in mind—most of the early cinemas were in facing
brickwork or reconstructed stone. Later, as new materials
became readily available and designers began to realise that
they were not necessarily building for posterity, less permanent finishes came into vogue. Colour was introduced into
large areas of the façades, and biscuit-coloured faience tiling,
terrazzo, terra-cotta used as a veneer, white pre-cast concrete slabs and black 'vitrolite' were among the new
materials introduced.

The Regal at Wimbledon by Robert Cromie is basically
a brick building but faced in a reconstructed stone with a
granite finish. Black faience columns were used between the
windows. Its appearance is solid and heavy but it has
weathered extremely well. This heaviness was echoed in
the Odeon at Weston-super-Mare by Cecil Howitt, but this
time quite a different use of material was made. The faceted
elevations were finished in amber and green faience tiles,
each 2 feet square, with broad parapets at the top. These

The Dreamland Cinema, Margate.
Architects: Julian Leathart

Opposite Stalls plan and cross-section of the Regal, Wimbledon.
Architect: Robert Cromie

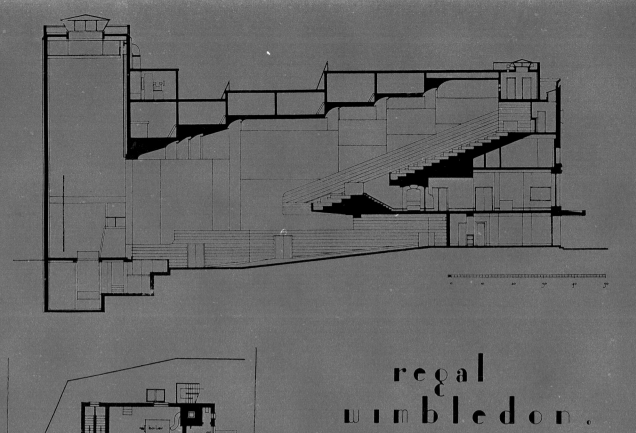

regal
wimbledon.

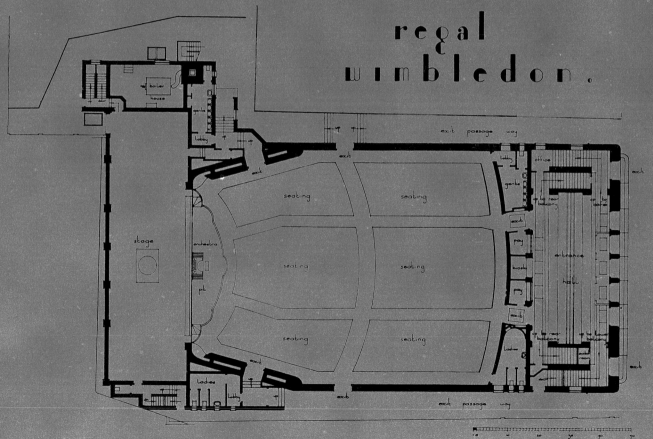

stage

orchestra
pit

seating

seating

seating

seating

seating

seating

boiler
house

gents

lobby

exit

exit

exit passage way

exit

lobby

gents

exit

pay

kiosk

pay

exit

office

up to rear
balcony

entrance

hall

up to front
balcony

exit

up to rear
balcony

up to front
balcony

exit

ladies

ladies

lobby

exit

exit passage way

stalls plan

parapets also had sunken bands of jade green tiles into which were set the continuous tubes of neon lighting. Below the canopy that projected over the entrance the columns were faced with black armoured plate glass panels fixed in silvered metal frames.

By the middle of the 'thirties architects were beginning to find, with so many new cinemas going up, that the functional and technical aspects of cinema design were becoming more standardised. There was no precise prototype such as the Ministry of Education has prepared for school buildings, but cinemas began to be built to a distinct pattern. The technical press included numerous features by leading architects on cinema design and construction, and this had a formative influence on work throughout the country.

The standard adopted for a super cinema seems to have been—except in the case of special buildings—an auditorium with a capacity of 1,600–2,000, concentric seating usually in banks of three, a stalls floor raked at an angle of 1 in 10, and an overall size for the building of about 120–180 feet long by 70–80 feet wide.

Small stages were popular with designers and this resulted in most cases in the elimination of fly towers together with the numerous dressing rooms that had been a feature of larger cinemas in the late 'twenties. Nearly all supers were built with balconies although many arguments were put forward for the further development of the stadium type. Kemp's Hereford Ritz was just such a development. Plans were consistently axial, with front walls splayed-in

towards the proscenium in almost every case. The only ceptions were where the architect was attempting to cr a total egg-shaped or fan-shaped volume (for exampl W E Trent's Gaumont, Finchley) or where the site res tions made a conventionally shaped auditorium imposs

In contrast to European practice all the pre-auditor space in English cinemas was placed, as it had bee theatre design earlier, in the front of the house. This the architect room to fit in his extra accommodation restaurants, dance halls and management offices on the floor, beneath the spread of the balcony and above entrance doors. Robert Cromie's Regal at Wimble clearly set the precedent for this.

In 1931 attempts were made to interest English cin architects in new ideas for the layout of auditoria base a parabolic reversed floor system pioneered by Schlanger and other cinema architects in the United St In this system the highest part of the floor was neares the screen and individual seats tilted slightly backward the reversed floor giving, it was claimed, better sight l It also ensured that the level of the balcony was much lo and less steep, thus providing the projectionist wit almost horizontal throw for the picture. It was an arra ment that could have totally changed the concept of cin design in this country. It demanded a close collabora between technicians and architects which in fact was forthcoming. Although it was not adopted in this cou

nglish architects kept rigidly to the concept of axial sight
es both in plan and in section) it was used successfully in
nerica and in the Victor Hugo Theatre in Paris, designed
Charavel and Melenides. An interesting experiment on
nilar lines, but with a double-raked auditorium floor, was
idertaken in South Africa, in the highly successful 20th
ntury Cinema, Johannesburg.

If English architects by and large were slow to accept
novations in planning and cinematographic techniques
ey made up for this in the common concern they displayed
r good acoustics and lighting. The need to provide good
ght lines was the basic premise on which the architect
signed his building. Sight angles were drawn on the very
st rough schemes and adhered to during the progress of
e design. The earlier difficulties encountered in the poor
finition and the limited throw of projectors had been
ercome and the sizing of auditoria during the super era
as based on well-founded technical information.

Lighting, on the other hand, was more pragmatic. The
splendent lighting schemes found in many British cinemas
veloped directly from the 'palaces of light' in America.
ior to 1930 colour lighting installations usually consisted
individual coloured bulbs operated from main switch-
ards housed in the basement or behind the stage area. At
e beginning of 1930 the semi-atmospheric Richmond
inema, designed by Leathart and Granger, was completed
corporating the latest Holophane magazine colour light-
g equipment. This created something of a revolution in

auditorium design. The automatically controlled system
developed by Holophane was refined and new colour effects
added in several cinemas such as the Capitol, Aberdeen, and
the Capitol, Didsbury. When the latter was rebuilt (having
been gutted by fire in 1933) an even more elaborate system
of colour-change lighting was installed. According to a contemporary report the results were sensational, with each
colour sequence changing every ten minutes and the whole
range of hues only becoming apparent after $3\frac{1}{2}$ hours.

Elsewhere lighting effects were following the pattern of
German examples such as the Titania-Palast in Berlin, and
the New Victoria in London. With the later marriage of
acoustics and lighting the plain curved ceiling with lighting
in troughs became a main feature of interiors. External
lighting also followed German practice. Night effects often
made an unattractive façade look impressive and even important in the street scene. Gaumont and Odeon cinemas
looked particularly well once ensconced in darkness. Many
others harked back to their fairground origins with garish
signs and neon tubes lacing the vertical and horizontal
motifs on the exterior.

Apart from the visual aspects cinema designers had to
provide expert knowledge on such matters as projection as
well as heating and ventilation. The operating box suite—
as the projection booth was known—has been called the
'nerve centre of the modern cinema'. Outside the public
view, it was treated quite differently from any other part of
the building. Stark interiors with plain walls and low ceilings

**Before and after the Inferno,
The Capitol, Didsbury,
Manchester**

characterised the operational centre. In the larger and mo
impressive buildings the projection suite was designed li
the operating theatre in a hospital, everything clearly la
out, lighting fitted over the machines, the projectors them
selves evenly spaced at the regulation distances on the ce
tral axis of the cinema. To one side of the projection roo
was situated the rewind and workrooms. The suite was com
pletely self-contained and had ready access to the open-ai

Heating and ventilation necessitated the provision
space in the basement or under the stage for the boiler hou
and chambers for the ventilating equipment. Full air con
ditioning was rare in English cinemas, the usual practi
being to install a plenum system that washed and warme

circulated air. Cinema owners were often proud of the
complex equipment used for this process and in a number
of cases the mechanical 'guts' of the building were displayed
to the general public through full-length ground-floor
windows along the sides of the heating chamber.

Interior decoration in English cinemas had four distinct
phases. Immediately after the First World War, Neo-
Grecian ornament was very much in vogue. The second
phase, which Julian Leathart has called the 'umbrella
period', was more adventurous. Under the umbrella were
sheltered and nurtured, the Chinese, Egyptian, Spanish,
Italian and Tottenham Court Road' styles. The third period

saw the introduction of Continental ideas, largely based on
French examples. Lastly, an attempt to come to terms with
the embryonic Modern Movement in its Germanic and
Dutch form can be seen on the part of certain progressive
English architects. This phase was represented by the
elimination of ostentatious and superficial ornament and
the introduction of smooth rectilinear or curved surfaces.
This last phase also saw a revival of brickwork treatment
(from the Dutch) and experimentation with the new surface materials and artificial stone panelling.

Chronologically, Leathart and Granger's Kensington
Cinema belongs to the 'twenties phase. It was stylistically
coherent, rooted in the detail and ornamentation of the Neo-

171

A wide choice of interior light
fittings was always available to
the designer in every conceivable
mode

Grec, but soon became dated. Leathart began to realise that certain architectural characteristics preferred in individual countries were gradually being abandoned. Referring to the Kensington in a paper to the Royal Institute of British Architects he said, 'It was opened five years ago, and, together with the recently opened New Victoria, demonstrated the extreme ends of the gamut of styles. It would be just as impossible to imagine a Kensington interior as suitable today as it would be for the Victoria to have been designed five years ago.' The developments that had taken place in acoustic design and in the use of concealed and coloured lighting changed completely the cinema interior. At the Kensington the design of the interior lighting relied for its effect entirely on visible points of illumination. The New Victoria was more in line with current German practice with decorative light sources and smoothly curved lighting troughs that gave rise to the rich forms of the interior.

The simple, clean lines and the undecorated surfaces that had been a feature of German and French cinemas for many years were only introduced in England after the stage-set ideas had run their course. Serge Chermayeff had successfully brought the real modern idiom to London (from France) when he eliminated all decorative overtones in his interior for the Cambridge Theatre in 1929.

After 1934, excluding the work of Komisarjevsky, the designers of cinemas in this country incorporated light sources within the general acoustic and decorative treatment, often concealing them in the coves and sconces which

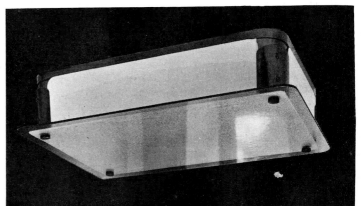

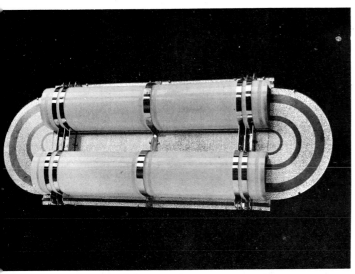

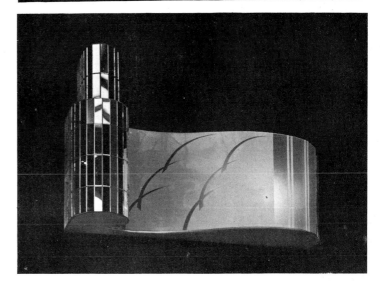

The nerve centre of a super cinema, the projection room

curved over the whole auditorium. It became the motif of the British cinema. It seems now to sum up aesthetically the whole era of the super cinema: modernistic, 'jazzy', with colour oozing from concealed sources, and the beam of light from the projector cutting through the haze from a hidden mechanical box of tricks.

Exterior design had also changed. The theatrical fronts in bourgeois Adam style had died long before, leaving the average architect with the problem of finding an adequate image for his own buildings. On the whole, in retrospect, it cannot be said that very many cinemas succeeded architecturally. Probably the widespread use of the dominant vertical tower contrasting with the long low horizontal box was too elementary. Apart from the obvious interest there was in the technical side of cinema design and the exchange of ideas between those members of the profession engaged on such work, the cynicism of the rest of their colleagues was obvious. It is not by chance that the official organ of the architectural profession in this country, *The Journal of the Royal Institute of British Architects,* did not feature a single cinema building in its pages during the years 1936–39. Even those actively engaged in the design of cinema buildings realised that for all their labours little architecture of any real importance emerged.

Robert Cromie, in an article in *Architectural Design and Construction* for March 1938, made a plea for the improvement of design standards in cinemas. 'With so many architects of the younger generation employed it is impossible to avoid remarking upon the rather low average skill a inventiveness in design generally.' He went on, 'every n cinema should improve its locality, and the individuality cities should be nurtured, not menaced, by such buildin Unfortunately this was not a view often shared by industry, as one can still see from the way cinemas have b sited and decorated in so many of our historic towns.

Cinema architecture, as Cromie pointed out, suffe from too rapid expansion, a fact that is reflected by the t hundred or so new buildings that went up in England 1937. The industry was running away with itself and arc tects were trying desperately to keep up with it. 'The arc tect's job', Cromie wrote, 'is so much of a struggle squeeze a quart into a pint, a week into a day, to mak hundred pounds produce a lot.'

Cromie goes on: 'Of all buildings none are more fascin ing to design, more difficult to construct nor more unsatis ing when built. . . . But there is no reason why ciner should not present in mien and form something of the co fortable elegance and repose of our best domestic work is strange that an industry which includes so many peo of artistic perception has not seen to this.' John Betjem had summed up the situation in 1935 when he wrote t the truly modern kinema has yet to be built in England' would be, he. said, a product of its age and not a ser mental reminder of another, 'dateless . . . as St Paul's, Parthenon and the Empire Swimming Pool, Wembl How right he was. It still has not appeared.